Landmarks of w

Baudelaire

LES FLEURS DU MAL

Landmarks of world literature

General Editor: J. P. Stern

BAUDELAIRE

Les Fleurs du Mal

F. W. LEAKEY

Emeritus Professor of French
University of London

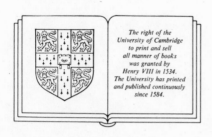

The right of the
University of Cambridge
to print and sell
all manner of books
was granted by
Henry VIII in 1534.
The University has printed
and published continuously
since 1584.

CAMBRIDGE UNIVERSITY PRESS

Cambridge
New York   Port Chester
Melbourne   Sydney

Published by the Press Syndicate of the University of Cambridge
The Pitt Building, Trumpington Street, Cambridge CB2 1RP
40 West 20th Street, New York, NY 10011-4211, USA
10 Stamford Road, Oakleigh, Victoria 3166, Australia

First published 1992

Printed in Great Britain at the University Press, Cambridge

A catalogue record for this book is available from the British Library

Library of Congress cataloguing in publication data

Leakey, F. W.
Baudelaire: Les Fleurs du Mal / F. W. Leakey.
    p.   cm. – (Landmarks of world literature)
Includes index.
ISBN 0 521 36116 8 (hardback) – ISBN 0 521 36937 1 (paperback)
1. Baudelaire, Charles, 1821–1867. Fleurs du Mal. I. Title.
II. Series.
PQ2191. F63L43 1992
841′ .8–dc20   91–19653   CIP

ISBN 0 521 36116 8 hardback
ISBN 0 521 36937 1 paperback

GG

Contents

Preface

Baudelaire's *Les Fleurs du Mal*, which used to be the most infamous book of poems in French literature, has in this century become the most famous, and the most admired; this development would surely have astounded his nineteenth-century contemporaries. But then the whole history of this book, from beginning to end, is shot through with paradox. *Les Fleurs du Mal* (which began life, in the 1840s and early 1850s, under two quite different titles: *Les Lesbiennes* and *Les Limbes*) earned its initial notoriety from the trial and judicial condemnation which followed its first publication in 1857; some ninety years later, in 1949, this condemnation was to be officially annulled by a judgment of the Supreme Court of Appeal in Paris. But this ultimate canonisation, both legal and literary, carries a further paradox. *Les Fleurs du Mal* now owes its true prestige, its true attainment of 'landmark' status, to the sheer aesthetic quality of its verses, and it is this above all, therefore, that we must study and appreciate; yet even today a lingering and piquant aura of scandal, of remembered bravado in a challenge to convention and authority, persists from that first publication.

I add a few explanatory notes concerning the present text. All Baudelaire references are to the companion two-volume editions by Claude Pichois of the *Œuvres complètes* and the *Correspondance* (both published by Gallimard, 'Bibliothèque de la Pléiade', 1975–6 and 1973 respectively; abbreviated *OCP* and *CPl*). *Les Fleurs du Mal*, with full documentary annotation and (on pp. 1581–91) an alphabetical index to the poems, is in the first volume of the *Œuvres complètes*. (For full details of all other books mentioned, see 'Guide to further reading'.) In providing English versions of the texts of Baudelaire's poems, I have chosen a composite and flexible

approach, combining more or less free translations, para-
phrases, summaries or simply amplified titles, as seemed
appropriate in each case; such a method best serves, in my
view, to convey to the English-speaking reader the sense,
imagery and vocabulary, in part or in full, of the original,
whilst avoiding the unidiomatic and stilted awkwardness that
so often afflicts even the best literal prose translations. (For
the question of verse translations, see pp. 100–3, below.) I
should finally mention that my fourth chapter, 'Swan-song',
has been adapted from my essay 'The Originality of *Le
Cygne*', as previously published in my *Baudelaire. Collected
Essays*, 1990, and that I have re-utilised, elsewhere also, other
and briefer passages from those same essays.

In conclusion, I must acknowledge my indebtedness firstly
to Andrew Macanulty, James Patty and Ted Taylor for the
bibliographical help they have given me; secondly and above
all to Peter Stern, for his helpful advice and comment on the
organisation of this book.

Chronology

	Biography	History, literature and the arts
1828	8 November. Remarriage of his mother, aged thirty-five, to the thirty-nine-year-old Major (eventually General) Aupick – whom Baudelaire came to regard, not unnaturally, as both an interloper and an enemy.	ADM (= Alfred de Musset), *L'Anglais mangeur d'opium* (free adaptation of De Quincey's *Confessions*). Sainte-Beuve, *Tableau de la poésie française au XVIe siècle.*
1829		Sainte-Beuve, *Vie, poésies et pensées de Joseph Delorme.* Hugo, *Les Orientales; Marion de Lorme.*
1830		27–9 July. Revolution: 'Journées de juillet: Les Trois Glorieuses'. 2 August. Abdication of Charles X. 9 August. Installation of Louis-Philippe as his successor. Musset, *Contes d'Espagne et d'Italie.*
1831	November. Aupick posted to Lyons, and appointed Chief of Staff of the 7th Division.	21-2 November. First uprising of the silk workers in Lyons. Hugo, *Les Feuilles d'automme.* Balzac, *La Peau de chagrin.*
1832	January. Baudelaire moves to Lyons with his mother, and is enrolled as a pupil, and later as a boarder, at the Collège royal.	

1833	→ 1835. Balzac, *Histoire des Treize* (including *La Fille aux yeux d'or*).
1834	April. The Collège royal, by virtue of its location, is indirectly involved in the silk-workers' uprising. Baudelaire's compassionate reaction to these events, though unrecorded at the time, finds utterance some seventeen years later, in → 1851, in his article on the Lyonnais poet, Pierre Dupont (*OCP* II, p. 31). Aupick promoted to the rank of Colonel, in part as a reward for his role in the repression of the uprising.	10–13 April. Second uprising of the silk workers in Lyons. Sainte-Beuve, *Volupté*. → 1835. Balzac, *Le Père Goriot*.
1835		Hugo, *Les Chants du crépuscule*. Vigny, *Chatterton*.
1836	January. Aupick appointed Chief of Staff to the 1st Military Division in Paris. Further Parisian commands follow in → 1840, 1841, 1842 and 1844. February. Baudelaire moves to Paris with his mother, and enters the Collège Louis-le-Grand as a boarder.	Musset, *La Confession d'un enfant du siècle*. Gautier, *Mademoiselle de Maupin*.
1837		Hugo, *Les Voix intérieures*.

Biography	History, literature and the arts
1838	Gautier, *La Comédie de la Mort.* Poe, *The Narrative of Arthur Gordon Pym.*
1839 18 April. Expulsion from the Collège Louis-le-Grand, in consequence of a culminating act of indiscipline. While pursuing (nominally) further academic studies from a *pension*, leads a 'vie libre' and gradually drifts into a recklessly dissolute way of life; by the autumn, has contracted venereal disease, and has begun to accumulate the debts from which he was unable thereafter ever to free himself. 12 August. Gains his baccalaureate (with some external help?); on the same day, Aupick promoted to be a Brigadier.	
1840	Poe, *Tales of the Arabesque and Grotesque.* Hugo, *Les Rayons et les ombres.* Musset, *Poésies complètes.* Sainte-Beuve, *Poésies complètes.*

1841 June. Alarmed as much by Baudelaire's resolve to become a writer as by the 'unhealthy relationships' into which he had fallen (and which seemed already to be reflected in his writings), Aupick despatches his stepson, as a remedial and disciplinary measure, on a long sea-voyage around the Cape of Good Hope, with Calcutta as the intended destination. September. Having reached the islands of Mauritius and Bourbon, Baudelaire refuses to travel any further and insists on taking the next boat home.

1842 16 February. Arrives back at Bordeaux. 28 April. Comes into his father's inheritance, sets up on his own, and to his stepfather's and mother's alarm seems bent on dilapidating as rapidly as possible the modest fortune he has acquired. Reaffirms his determination to become a writer, and shortly after takes as his mistress a coloured girl, Jeanne Duval, thereby embarking upon a long, stormy and poetically fruitful relationship which (unlike others, more transient or unsuccessful) was to persist in one form or another → into the early 1860s.

Posthumous publication of Aloysius Bertrand's prose poems, *Gaspard de la nuit*. Banville, *Les Cariatides*.

	Biography	*History, literature and the arts*
1843	May. Publication of the collective volume *Vers*, to which initially he himself was to have contributed, and of which the ultimate joint authors are his friends since 1840, Le Vavasseur, Prarond and Dozon.	Balzac, *Illusions perdues*.
	October. Moves to the most famous of his innumerable lodgings, the Hôtel Pimodan (later, the Hôtel Lauzen), where he remains until → September 1845.	
1844	August–September. His financial situation being deemed by his family to have reached crisis point, a 'conseil judiciaire' or legal guardian is appointed in the person of the solicitor Ancelle; from that time onwards, Baudelaire becomes a 'remittance man', eking out a monthly allowance with gifts from his mother and with endless borrowings (mostly never repaid). Immediately, and no doubt as a gesture of protest to mark his severance from his family, he takes on for nearly three and a half years, until → January 1848, various literary pseudonyms ('Baudelaire-Dufaÿs', etc.) derived from his mother's maiden surname.	Vigny, *La Maison du berger*, in the *Revue des Deux Mondes*.

1845
Mid-May. *Salon de 1845* (a review of the annual Paris art exhibition): his first publication under his own name, and the first testimony of his lifelong admiration for Delacroix.

25 May. First published poem, in *L'Artiste: A une [dame] créole* ('To a Creole Lady').

30 June. Suicide attempt: although not without burlesque elements, this is a genuine cry for help from one trapped, as his letter to Ancelle of that date reveals (*CPI* I, pp. 124–6), in despair and self-disgust.

October. First announcement of his projected volume of poems, *Les Lesbiennes*; further announcements will follow in → 1846–7.

Poe, *The Raven, and Other Poems; Tales of Mystery and Imagination*.
De Quincey, 'Suspiria de Profundis' (additional last part of *Confessions of an English Opium-Eater*), in *Blackwood's Magazine*.
Gautier, *Poésies complètes* (including *España*).
Wagner, *Tannhäuser*: first performance, Dresden.

1846
Early May. *Salon de 1846*: unlike its more conventional predecessor of 1845, this is a thinly disguised (and brilliant) aesthetic treatise.

10 May. Death of the artist Emile Deroy (Baudelaire's close friend and aesthetic mentor).
Banville, *Les Stalactites*.

1847   January. 'La Fanfarlo', in the *Bulletin de la Société des gens de lettres*: a semi-autobiographical novella, with references to many as yet unpublished poems. 22 April: Aupick promoted to rank of General; 28 November: appointed Head of the Ecole poly-technique.
During this year probably, Baudelaire becomes addicted to opium – taken initially, in the form of laudanum, as an analgesic and relaxant.

1848   January. Reviewing a collection of tales by Champfleury, reverts to his former signature 'Charles Baudelaire'.
February. On the outbreak of the Revolution, becomes a Republican sympathiser, is seen 'on the barricades' and helps to edit a short-lived newspaper, *Le Salut public*.
13 April. Aupick appointed, by the new Republican government, Ambassador in Constantinople.
15 July. In *La Liberté de penser*, 'Révélation magnétique' – the first of Baudelaire's long series of translations from Edgar Allan Poe.
November. First announcement, in an obscure journal of the wine trade, of the forthcoming publication of his poems under a new title, *Les Limbes*. Further announcements, accompanying or within texts of his own, follow in → 1850, 1851 and 1852.

22–4 February. 'Journées de février': abdication of Louis-Philippe; proclamation of the Second Republic.
22 June. Dissolution of the National Workshops.
23–6 June. 'Journées de juin': suppression of proletarian revolt.
10 December. Election of Louis-Napoleon as Prince-President of the Second Republic.

1849	7 October. Death of Edgar Allan Poe.
1850	18 August. Death of Balzac.
1851	2 December. *Coup d'état:* seizure of power by Louis-Napoleon. 21 December. National plebiscite, whereby Louis-Napoleon gains approval for his new Constitution. Murger, *Scènes de la vie de Bohème* (evokes the same world of Baudelaire's friends as → Champfleury's *Les Aventures de Mademoiselle Mariette*, 1853).

1851 7–12 March. 'Du Vin et du hachish' (first version of → *Les Paradis artificiels*, 1860) in *Le Messager de l'assemblée.*
9 April. 'Les Limbes' (a selection of eleven unpublished sonnets from the projected volume of this title) in *Le Messager de l'assemblée.*
18 June. Aupick, having returned from Constantinople, goes next to Madrid as Ambassador. October–November. Baudelaire shows Asselineau (his future biographer, now to become his close friend) the manuscript of *Les Limbes,* 'magnificently' copied out for him by a professional calligrapher; this manuscript will serve eventually as the basis for the printing, in → 1857, of *Les Fleurs du Mal.*

Biography

1852   After the political disillusions of December 1851, comes increasingly under the influence of Poe, in whom he sees a 'twin soul' and whose *Tales* he begins comprehensively to translate; having flirted briefly with utilitarianism in two essays, on 'Pierre Dupont' (August 1851) and 'L'Ecole païenne' (January 1852), he moves towards a strongly anti-didactic and 'purist' aesthetic, and on political and social questions takes up an increasingly reactionary standpoint.

March and April. 'Edgar Allan Poe, sa vie et ses ouvrages', in the *Revue de Paris*.

9 December. Sends anonymously to Mme Sabatier the manuscript, under an earlier title, of *A Celle qui est trop gaie* ('To the Too-Joyous One'); six further anonymous poems follow, the last being dated → 8 May 1854.

1853   8 March. Aupick, on his return from Madrid, is nominated a senator. He acquires, as a summer residence, the so-called 'Maison-joujou', or 'Toy House', at Honfleur.

History, literature and the arts

2 November. Second plebiscite: Louis-Napoleon gains recognition for the establishment of the Second Empire.

2 December. Official proclamation of the Second Empire.

Gautier, *Emaux et camées*.

Leconte de Lisle, *Poèmes antiques*.

June. Haussmann becomes Prefect of the Seine, and begins systematic reconstruction of the city of Paris.

Champfleury, *Les Aventures de Mademoiselle Mariette*, in which Baudelaire figures as 'le poète ami des chats'.

Hugo, *Châtiments*: satirical poems directed, from exile in the Channel Islands, against Louis-Napoleon and the Second Empire.

1854   → Summer 1855. Unsuccessfully woos the actress Marie Daubrun.

1855   26 May, 3 June and 12 August. Returns to art criticism with three articles on the *Exposition universelle*: 'Méthode de critique'; 'Eugène Delacroix'; 'Ingres'.
1 June. 'Les Fleurs du Mal', in the *Revue des Deux Mondes*. Eighteen poems – his most substantial verse publication so far; the book's definitive title here appears for the first time.
Probably during this year, draft article, 'Puisque réalisme il y a', in which Baudelaire attacks Courbet, Champfleury and the new Realist aesthetic.

26 January. Nerval (Baudelaire's friend, and the inspirer in 1844 and original dedicatee of the poem *Un voyage à Cythère*) found hanged, no doubt by his own hand, in a Parisian street. May–November. Paris Universal Exhibition. Courbet, whose paintings have been refused by the Jury, sets up a rival, 'Realist' exhibition of his own – which includes a painting, *L'Atelier du peintre* ('The Painter's Studio'), in which Baudelaire figures.

1856   12 March. *Histoires extraordinaires* (first published volume of his translations of Poe's *Tales*). Four further volumes follow in → 1857, 1858, 1863, 1865.

October–December. Advance publication, in the *Revue de Paris*, of Flaubert's *Madame Bovary*. Hugo, *Les Contemplations*.

1857   27 April. Death of General Aupick. Baudelaire's mother takes up permanent residence at Honfleur.
21 June. Publication of *Les Fleurs du Mal*.
17 July. Following hostile review in *Le Figaro*, the Public Prosecutor commits for trial Baudelaire, his publisher and his printer, and all copies of the book

29 January and 7 February. Trial (on charges of offending against 'public and religious morality and accepted standards') and acquittal of Flaubert and the *Revue de Paris*. Banville, *Odes funambulesques*.

Biography

are ordered to be confiscated. A number of
Baudelaire's friends, including Asselineau, rally to
his support; their published or unpublished articles
are collected in mid-August under the title *Articles
justificatifs pour Charles Baudelaire.*

August–September. Abortive affair with Mme.
Sabatier. Now revealed as the author of the seven
poems sent anonymously to her in 1852–4,
Baudelaire seeks her intervention on his behalf in the
impending legal battle; he is taken aback by the
ardour of her response, and the two retreat, by
mutual agreement, into what henceforth will be a
purely friendly relationship.

20 August. Trial of *Les Fleurs du Mal.* The Court,
having imposed fines on Baudelaire, his publisher
and his printer, orders six poems–(the so-called
'pièces condamnées'), deemed 'offensive to public
morals and accepted standards', to be excluded from
any future edition of the book.

24 August. First collective publication, in *Le
Présent*, of (six) prose poems, under the title
'Poèmes nocturnes'. Further publications follow,
under various alternative titles, in → 1861, 1862,
1863, 1864 and 1866.

18 October. Baudelaire reviews, in *L'Artiste,*
Flaubert's *Madame Bovary*, now published in book
form.

1858	21 October. Pays the first of a whole series of visits, extending → over the next two years, to Honfleur; at certain moments, has the vain hope of installing himself there with his mother. End-1858 → mid-1860: period of renewed poetic creativity, centred on Honfleur.	
1859	10 and 20 June, 1 and 20 July. 'Salon de 1859', in the *Revue française.* August–November. Renewed (and again unsuccessful) attempt to woo Marie Daubrun. Early November. Publication by Poulet-Malassis of *Théophile Gautier*, with preface by Victor Hugo, in which the latter applies to Baudelaire the famous formula: 'Vous créez un frisson nouveau'.	8 December. Death of Thomas de Quincey. Hugo, *La Légende des siècles* I.
1860	13 January. First cerebral stroke. 17 February. Addresses an admiring letter to Wagner, after attending the latter's concerts at the Théâtre-Italien. End-May. *Les Paradis artificiels.*	25 January, 1 and 8 February. Wagner conducts three orchestral and choral concerts of his music at the Théâtre-Italien.

1861   Early February. Publication by Poulet-Malassis of second edition of *Les Fleurs du Mal* (with the six 'pièces condamnées' duly excised, but with an additional thirty-two poems).

13 March. First of three performances only, at the Opéra, of Wagner's *Tannhäuser.*

13 March. Attends first performance of *Tannhäuser,* at the Opéra.

1 April. 'Richard Wagner', in the *Revue européenne.* End-April. *Richard Wagner et 'Tannhäuser' à Paris* (publication in booklet form of the article of 1 April, with an addendum: 'Encore quelques mots', taking account of the performances of the opera in March).

11 December. Actively contemplates putting himself forward as a candidate for the Académie française; finally withdraws → 10 February 1862.

1862   23 January. Records, in an entry in one of his 'Intimate Journals' (*OCP* I, p. 668), having received a dire 'warning', relative to his perennial feeling of giddiness: in his own words, he feels passing over him 'the wind of the wing of imbecility'.

Hugo, *Les Misérables.*

14 April. Death at Fontainebleau of his half-brother, Claude-Alphonse – of the same cause as later brought about Baudelaire's own death: hemiplegic paralysis.

Mid-July. Publication of volume IV (devoted to nineteenth-century authors) of Eugène Crépet's anthology, *Les Poètes français.* Seven of the

introductory articles (those on Hugo, Gautier, Banville, Leconte de Lisle, and on three others) are by Baudelaire; the 'Notice' on Baudelaire himself is by Gautier.
6 September. Swinburne, eulogistic review in *The Spectator* of the second edition of *Les Fleurs du Mal*.

1863   2 September, 14 and 22 November. 'L'Œuvre et la vie d'Eugène Delacroix' – obituary article in *L'Opinion nationale*.
End-September. Poulet-Malassis obliged, by his bankruptcy in ← 1862, to flee to Brussels and relinquish his right to publish works by Baudelaire.
26 and 29 November, 3 December. 'Le Peintre de la vie moderne' (essay, in *Le Figaro*, on the draughtsman and water-colourist Constantin Guys, here unnamed; composed ← 1859–61).

13 August. Death of Delacroix.
17 September. Death of Vigny.
October. 'Salon des Refusés': exhibition of paintings refused by the official Salon; includes famous canvas, 'Le Déjeuner sur l'herbe', by Baudelaire's friend Manet.

1864   24 April. Arrives in Brussels, in fulfilment of plans first projected over eight months previously, to give a series of public readings, in May and June, from his articles on Delacroix and Gautier and from *Les Paradis artificiels*.

Biography

1865 → 1866. Increasingly the victim of illness: neuralgia, stomach cramps, rheumatism, fevers, giddiness, nausea, etc.

1866 End-February or early March. Publication by Poulet-Malassis in 'Amsterdam' (i.e. Brussels) of *Les Epaves*, 'Relics': twenty-three poems, including the six 'pièces condamnées', the poem in Latin *Franciscae meae laudes* ('In Praise of my Françoise'), and sixteen further poems which had not appeared in either the 1857 or 1861 editions of *Les Fleurs du Mal*.

Around 15 March. After a fall in the church of Saint-Loup in Namur, apoplexy and aphasia set in, together with hemiplegic paralysis on the right side. 29 June. Transported from Brussels to a nursing home in Paris. He survives physically, if not intellectually, for a further → 14 months, thanks to the care of his mother and his friends.

October. *Le Parnasse contemporain* (collection in book form of periodical publications of new verse) reprints from its March and July numbers sixteen of his poems, fifteen of them under the title 'Nouvelles Fleurs du Mal'.

History, literature and the arts

1 February. Mallarmé, 'Symphonie littéraire', in *L'Artiste* (part 2: eulogy of Baudelaire). 16 and 30 November, 23 December. In *L'Art*, enthusiastic articles by Verlaine on Baudelaire (who did not appreciate them; see *CPl* II, pp. 625, 626, 972).

1867 31 August. Death.
      2 September, Funeral, and burial (in the family
      vault) at the Cimetière Montparnasse; the memorial
      speeches are heard by around sixty people. His
      'jinx', his *guignon* (the title of one of his poems),
      pursues him to the end: as Claude Pichois and Jean
      Ziegler remark (*Baudelaire*, p. 593), he dies
      'inconveniently', on a Saturday in midsummer . . .

Chapter 1

Composition

The poet in a bourgeois era

The first French Revolution of 1789 saw the emergence of the middle classes as a political and economic force, in opposition to the aristocracy; but the consolidation of that power, after a succession of régimes (the First Republic: Convention, Directory, Consulate; Napoleon's First Empire; the restored Bourbon monarchy in 1814), came only in 1830, with the coronation of Louis-Philippe after a second Revolution. That 'bourgeois monarchy' lasted only until 1848, but the new organisation of society survived in broad terms a Second Republic (1848–52), a Second Empire under Louis-Napoleon (1852–70), a Third Republic lasting into our own century.

The coming of a bourgeois era posed new problems for the artist in general and the poet in particular. Romanticism, as an aesthetic movement, postulated the intellectual and spiritual primacy of the creative artist; no such primacy or economic security, however, was accorded him within the bourgeois scheme, and moreover he often offended against conventional moral standards. Within Romantic mythology, and that of subsequent aesthetic movements, too, the bourgeois thus became an enemy and the poet a beleaguered victim, sadly, 'unacknowledged' as (in Shelley's terms) the 'legislator of the world' his unique gifts qualified him to be.

This highly generalised picture obviously needs correction in respect of individual cases. Lamartine, for instance, did attain political authority in 1848, as effective Head for a few months of the Provisional Government of the Second Republic; Hugo drew substantial financial rewards from all

1

his writings, including his poems, and gained enormous prestige and popularity in exile under the Second Empire and thereafter under the Third Republic; Baudelaire himself, though for most of his life violently opposed to conventional morality, attempted briefly and opportunistically to come to terms with his bourgeois public in 1845–6 (see my *Baudelaire*, pp. 183–90, 'The wooing of the bourgeois'). The nineteenth century nevertheless certainly had its poet-victims; Baudelaire in particular, in the light of the *Fleurs du Mal* trial of 1857, becomes a special case, suffering active persecution at the hands of a hypocritical bourgeois establishment, and in that context inviting analogy with the admired poet–martyrs of previous centuries – with the sixteenth-century Tasso of Delacroix's paintings, the eighteenth-century Chatterton of Vigny's Romantic drama of that name.

A young man's book

The first thing to understand about *Les Fleurs du Mal*, is that it is essentially a young man's book; though published when Baudelaire was in his mid-thirties, in 1857, the poems it contained had in fact largely been written, at least in first draft, when he was still in his early twenties, during the period 1841–6 when, against his family's wishes, he had embarked upon his literary career. An initial study of the book's composition – a word we need to take here in both its senses: 'content' as well as 'genesis' – will serve not only to explain the seemingly interminable delays which impeded publication of the book, but also to clarify Baudelaire's intentions when he was finally able to present it to his readers, in a very different arrangement from the one originally envisaged.

A first chance for Baudelaire to publish perhaps as many as forty of his poems, came to him in the early months of 1843, when, with his friends Le Vavasseur, Prarond and Dozon, he prepared to bring out a collective volume under the studiedly neutral title *Vers*. At the last minute, however, he withdrew from this project – no doubt partly because of his sensitiveness to certain criticisms made of the poems he submitted, but perhaps also because of his own dissatisfaction with these poems, as reflected in a uniquely searching document of youthful self-criticism, the novella *La Fanfarlo* (composed 1843–6, published at the beginning of 1847).

Les Lesbiennes (1845–7)

In 1845, the year of Baudelaire's first published work under his own name, the *Salon de 1845*, came the promise of a collection of poems entirely by him, to be called *Les Lesbiennes*. From this 'firecracker' title − altogether more challenging than the anodyne *Vers*; for the description 'titre pétard', see *CPl* I, p. 378 − it seems certain that Baudelaire's book would have included in an eponymous first section, probably designed originally as a verse novel, the three Lesbian poems which eventually figure in the *Fleurs du Mal* of 1857; other poems in other sections would no doubt have been added to fill out the 'large-quarto' volume, but it is impossible without further evidence to say exactly which these might have been − the more so since Baudelaire, to judge by the oblique comments made on his earlier poems in *La Fanfarlo*, seems at that date to have been dissatisfied with many of these.

Les Limbes (1848–52)

The *Lesbiennes* project never of course materialised − mainly no doubt because of Baudelaire's desperate personal circumstances (moral as well as material) during the year 1847. From that low-water mark he was rescued by the Revolution of February 1848, which for a while swept him, like so many writers and artists of the time, into the politically active ranks of the Republicans and Socialists. Even more important for us, it led him to devise, under the title *Les Limbes*, an entirely new and ideologically acceptable framework for the publication of *all* the poems he had thus far composed and felt able to avow − rather than some only of these, as in the case of *Les Lesbiennes*. There could of course be no question, in this new phase of political and journalistic activity into which he had thrown himself, of his settling down afresh to compose a further collection of suitably socialist and humanitarian poems; his inspired solution, therefore, since these earlier verses constituted his sole available poetic capital, was to present them as it were objectively; rather than as an expression of his own personal ideas, these earlier verses could be seen as a sort of collective chronicle of the troubled feelings of a whole youthful generation. But the new title (now 'mysterious' rather than of 'firecracker' type; see again *CPl* I, p. 378) clearly also has its significance: modern youth, for Baudelaire, seems caught as if in a time-warp, in an uncertain transitional zone between the old world and the new, reminiscent of that theological *limbo* in which souls after death await their final redemption.

The complete manuscript of *Les Limbes*, as shown by Baudelaire to Asselineau in October or November 1851, has unfortunately disappeared; what have survived, however, are the texts of some twenty-seven poems extracted from that manuscript – which we know moreover, again from Asselineau, to have included all the poems which were to figure in *Les Fleurs du Mal* some six years later, together with a number of additional pieces which Baudelaire decided to 'sacrifice' (his words) at that date. From the titles and subjects of the last two sections of the 1857 *Fleurs du Mal*: 'Le Vin' and 'La Mort', we may gather that these sections will already have figured as such in *Les Limbes*; so perhaps also did the first and third sections of the 1857 edition: 'Spleen et Idéal' and 'Révolte'.

Les Fleurs du Mal (1857)

Although, in 1852, Baudelaire's *Limbes* project may have seemed so near to realisation, several factors conspired at that time to prevent him from carrying it through. Political, first of all: after the *coup d'état* of December 1851, his scheme will no longer have seemed to him, let alone to others, to provide an acceptable framework for his verses – even though later developments (those of 1855–7) were to show that these same poems could well be presented in a quite different and un-political light. Circumstantial, next: by ill-chance, another verse collection, bearing the same title, had come out (however obscurely, in Poitiers) in May 1852. Above all, creative: in that same year, his growing enthusiasm for Edgar Allan Poe determined him on a new career as the accredited translator of the American writer's works — the presenter to the French public of this great but too little-known foreign genius. This decisive commitment to Poe — which incidentally, was to bring him his greatest and most secure contemporary fame, and the sole substantial financial rewards for his writings he was ever to enjoy — did not, even in 1852, cause him to abandon entirely his efforts to place his own poems, nor his hope that in collected form they might eventually find a publisher. But for really serious progress to be made in this direction, Baudelaire had to await an important event which occurred towards the end of 1854: the inspired suggestion made at that time by Hippolyte Babou that his friend's book should henceforth bear the title 'Les Fleurs du Mal'. Almost immediately after this, Baudelaire entered into protracted negotiations with the *Revue des Deux Mondes*, as a result of which that highly respectable and influential journal agreed to publish on 1 June 1855, under the new-found title, a full eighteen of his poems — selected, of course, from the two albums previously destined for *Les Limbes*.

This publication in the *Revue des Deux Mondes* was highly important for Baudelaire — not only because it for the first time brought a considerable amount of his poetry before a wider public, but above all because the selection included so many texts of the very highest quality. Of further interest also is the principle Baudelaire sought to adopt (*CPl* I, p. 312) in the arrangement of these poems — that of *sequence*, with one poem leading smoothly into the next; this principle is one that he was able eventually to follow in his own distribution of his poems in the complete editions of 1857 and 1861.

At the end of 1856, Baudelaire at last found, in his pro-vidential friend Poulet-Malassis, a sympathetic publisher for the book under its new title; a contract between the two was

signed at the end of 1856, and at the beginning of the following February the poet set to work once again on the
manuscript previously prepared for *Les Limbes* — pruning
the poems down to an exact 100 (or rather 101, if the
prefatory *Au Lecteur*, 'To the Reader', is counted), by
'sacrificing' a number which had figured previously in the
Limbes manuscript; rearranging the chosen poems in accord-
ance with the new title and revised scheme that this entailed;
aiming assiduously at that uniform excellence and maximum
'conspicuousness' he had already proclaimed (*CPl* I, p. 364)
as the chief objective to be aimed at; above all, meticulously
revising each text through endless galley-proofs and page-
proofs, to the exasperation of his long-suffering publisher if
(more or less!) to his own ultimate satisfaction. For
understandable reasons, of course, as no doubt already
previously in his *Limbes* manuscript, Baudelaire was careful
to withhold all details as to the far distant dates of original
composition of his poems; not for him the precise — or ostensibly precise — chronology provided by Victor Hugo, say, in
his regular verse-collections of the same whole period.

In the volume as finally published by Poulet-Malassis on 21
June 1857, Baudelaire's 100 poems, following the verse preface
Au Lecteur, are grouped into five main sections: 'Spleen et
Idéal'; 'Fleurs du Mal', 'Révolte'; 'Le Vin'; 'La Mort'. The
first, third, fourth and fifth of these sections will no doubt have
been largely identical, as I have suggested, with those figuring
previously in *Les Limbes*; there is now, however, one highly important difference of *presentation* that Baudelaire was to
clarify (or confess), some nine years later, in a crucial and
movingly candid letter to his legal guardian Ancelle:

Must I then spell out to you, who have no more guessed it than has
anyone else, that into this *terrible* book I have poured my whole
heart, my whole *tenderness*, my whole *religion* (however travestied),
my whole *hatred*? It's true that I may assert the contrary, that I may
swear before high Heaven that the book is one of *pure art*, of *buf-
foonery*, of *jugglery* — and I shall be lying, lying in my teeth.

(*CPl* II, p. 610)

This subjective content, if not particularly brought out in the

Fleurs du Mal of 1857, no longer needed to be concealed
entirely from view − as will previously have been the case in
those heady days of 1848–51 when Baudelaire had felt obliged
(or had attempted) to reconcile his verses with the
Republican/Socialist ideology and intermittently utilitarian
aesthetic he then professed.

The arrangement Baudelaire devised for his poems in 1857
needs to be studied in some detail, since we know him to have
attached great importance to this − retrospective though it
may have been. The first of the five main sections is
disproportionately massive, including as it does nearly four-
fifths of all the poems within the book; under the conveniently
vague title 'Spleen et Idéal', we have in effect a sort of *om-
nium gatherum*, into which Baudelaire collected all the poems
that eluded classification into the other four more distinct
categories. (The order of words in the title, was clearly dic-
tated by euphony rather than literal accuracy − which would
have demanded, rather, 'Idéal et Spleen'.) Baudelaire does,
of course, make certain further groupings *within* the first
section of his book: thus a first sub-division (poems I–XI, in
the 1857 numbering; see *OCP* I, pp. 822–5) concerns the
creative artist − his place in society, his aspirations, his struggles, his achievements. In three only of these poems, nos. I,
IV and VI, is the theme general rather than personal; in all
the others Baudelaire speaks in his own name, and this
preponderance of the subjective over the objective is maintained in the succeeding texts − to become entire, of course,
in the thirty-six love poems (XX–LV) which form the largest
group in this section and indeed in the whole book. These love
poems − preceded by three sonnets, nos. XVII–XIX, pro-
claiming less purely erotic ideals of feminine or feminised
beauty − are interestingly grouped by Baudelaire according
to three main favoured 'types', associated (though not ex-
clusively) with particular women he had loved: a coloured
girl, of exotic origins and predatory disposition (Jeanne
Duval); a more mature woman, admired not always
platonically for her moral influence as well as for her joyous
radiance (Mme Sabatier); a buxom, childlike creature, finally,

of sometimes ambivalent temperament, from whom also emotional as well as physical consolation is sought (Marie Daubrun). As to why exactly Baudelaire should have chosen to group his poems in this manner, I would suggest that he was here consciously emulating the admired Ronsard, who three centuries earlier had himself produced three magnificent books of separately dedicated love lyrics: the *Amours de Cassandre*, the *Second Livre des Amours*, the *Sonnets pour Hélène*. In the 1857 *Fleurs du Mal*, Baudelaire's own set of miniature *canzoniere* is almost immediately followed by seven poems (LVIII–LXIV) which correspond to the first element in the sectional title ('Spleen et Idéal'), with four in particular (LIX–LXII) being specifically entitled *Spleen*. (For Baudelaire's personal interpretation of this term borrowed from the English, see p. 23, below.) As for the final, more miscellaneous, group of poems which closes the whole 'Spleen et Idéal' section, this includes a series of six, nos. LXV–LXX, which all share an urban or near-urban setting foreshadowing the 'Tableaux parisiens' group to be added in the *Fleurs du Mal* of 1861.

The second section, unlike the other four, cannot possibly have figured as such in the *Limbes* manuscript of 1849–52, since its eponymous title, 'Fleurs du Mal', clearly derives from the definitive naming of Baudelaire's book at the end of 1854. This does not mean, far from it, that the poems forming this section were all newly composed; on the contrary, nine of these twelve texts are specifically known to have existed before 1845, and the other three (nos. LXXXVI–LXXXVII and LXXXXIX), dating no doubt from the same period, will equally have been quarried from the 'Spleen et Idéal' or 'Révolte' sections of *Les Limbes*. The theme which unites these previously disparate but now linked poems, is not so much evil in general as, more particularly, sexual rebellion, enslavement and humiliation, his own and that of others. The next section dramatises a 'Révolte' which is explicitly religious, not to say blasphemous: St Peter is judged to have been entirely *right* to have denied Jesus, Cain is firmly preferred to Abel, Satan to God. The last two sections of the book, concerning Wine and Death respectively, are those in which the scheme devised for *Les Limbes* most obviously persists. In each of these two sections Baudelaire offers a mainly consoling poetic voice to various named social groups; in the final section of all, significantly, Death appears in that wholly 'friendly' guise (*Der Tod als Freund*) in which he is represented in an engraving by a contemporary German artist much admired by Baudelaire, Alfred Rethel.

So much for Baudelaire's grouping or overt classification of his poems − but there is also the principle (invoked already in connection with the *Revue des Deux Mondes* selection of 1855) of sequential continuity from one poem to another. A close examination of the 1857 edition, would show how extensively as well as ingeniously Baudelaire here contrived sequences of this kind. Here are four at least of the most striking such transitions: from the prefatory *Au Lecteur* to *Bénédiction* (the preponderant place of *ennui* in the world); from *Elévation* to *Correspondances* (the poet's, and Man's, apprehension of the language of Nature); from one animal species admired by the sage, to another − from *Les Chats* (favoured equally by lovers and scholars) to the owls of *Les Hiboux* (those models of unperturbed repose); from one lovers' paradise on earth, in *Le Vin des amants* ('The Lovers' Wine'), to another in Heaven, in *La Mort des amants* ('Death of the Lovers').

Baudelaire was well aware, in preparing his book for publication, that he risked prosecution on two grounds − for blasphemy and for 'offences against public morality'; these same charges were indeed being levelled at that very moment against Flaubert for his *Madame Bovary*. Of the various precautionary measures Baudelaire adopted to ward off these threats, one at least was to prove effective: this was the elaborate and avowedly 'destestable' note (*OCP* I, pp. 1075–6) prefixed to the 'Révolte' section, in which he explains that he is only affecting to espouse anti-religious opinions − those of 'ignorant' and 'angry' rebels − which of course he is far from sharing . . . Of the other three expedients he adopted, the first two had figured already in the *Revue des Deux Mondes* selection of 1855: a six-line epigraph taken from D'Aubigné's sixteenth-century epic poem, *Les Tragiques*, carrying the message that vice needed to be brought out into the open, rather than hidden away; a prefatory poem, *Au Lecteur*, which in effect implicated the reader in its catalogue of *universal* sin, and even, in its final line ('Hypocrite lecteur, – mon semblable, – mon frère!'), offered a sardonic anticipation of Hugo's classic defence of Romantic subjectivism, to *his* reader, in the prose preface of his *Contemplations* of 1856: 'How can you fail to understand that when I speak to you of myself, it is of *you* that I am speaking?' Baudelaire's third strategic precaution was adopted only at the very last moment: his addition, to the first of the two *Femmes damnées* poems ('Women damned'), of five thunderous concluding stanzas which transformed Delphine and Hippolyte into 'lamentable victims' inescapably bound for eternal damnation. But this last piecemeal measure proved to be no more than cosmetic: at the trial of 20 August 1857, the six poems ordered to be excised from any future edition of the book, as being likely to 'excite the senses' of its readers and to offend their sense of decency, included precisely the recently moralised *Femmes damnées* text – the other five being *Les Bijoux* ('The Jewels'), *Le Léthé*, *A celle qui est trop gaie*, *Lesbos* and *Les Métamorphoses du vampire* ('Transformations of a Vampire'). What seems curiously to have decided Baudelaire's fate as far as the six 'pièces condamnées' were concerned – and this is surely a significant indication of the 'moral standards' operative under the Second Empire – was that in these particular poems he had dared to describe in words what for centuries had been openly displayed in paintings: the female nude.

In the light of the book's previous history, it is interesting to examine the defence offered for it at the trial. Obviously Baudelaire felt obliged to make the case he felt most likely to be accepted by the Court; what he now claimed, therefore, was that from the book *taken as a whole* there emerged a 'terrible morality'; more specifically, he argued that the blasphemous or obscene poems needed to be set against others of a spiritual or platonic nature − such as *Bénédiction*, no doubt, or *Que diras-tu ce soir* . . . ('What message will you have for her tonight . . .?'), or *Le Flambeau vivant* ('The Living Torch'). What is nowhere claimed by either Baudelaire or his defence counsel, but only by his well-intentioned friend Barbey d'Aurevilly (who will doubtless have wrongly conflated two independent statements of the poet's), is that the book could only properly be understood in terms of its 'secret architecture' − that is, from the supposed total message that emerges from a consecutive reading, from the first page to the last, of all the poems in the book (a procedure more appropriate to a novel or a play, one would think, than to a collection of individual and separate lyric pieces!). But this whole moral defence of Baudelaire's was in any case soon to be discarded; we hear no more of it after 1857, though what does remain with him is his abiding concern for the *presentation* of his poems − for their careful grouping by themes and their sequential relation one with another.

Les Fleurs du Mal (1861)

Baudelaire's immediate reaction to the trial was one of dejection and deflation; he recognised his moral commitment, so to speak, to replace the six 'pièces condamnées' by other poems of equal or greater merit, yet believing his creative impulse as a poet to have altogether waned, he at first felt the task to be quite beyond him. He was rescued from this inertia, and enabled triumphantly to complete within four years a second edition of *Les Fleurs du Mal* which in many respects is far superior to the original one, by two fortunate discoveries: that the poems 'sacrificed' at the beginning of 1857 to make a taut and 'slimmed-down' first edition, were after all still ready to hand, for possible future exploitation or 'cannibalisation'; further, that the supposedly lost creative impulse *could* somehow be revived and galvanised, given a suitable new stimulus. This stimulus was happily provided by the 'Maison-joujou' at Honfleur, which had now become Mme Aupick's permanent home, and to which Baudelaire

made a number of creatively profitable visits between the end
of 1858 and the middle of 1860; one must allow also, perhaps,
for a certain obstinate, almost contra-suggestible resilience in
his temperament, which chose this moment to reassert itself
in the face of adversity. Thus it was that Baudelaire, after a
bleak year or so, finally found himself able, during the succeeding eighteen-month period, to compose or at least work
up from pre-existing fragments a further twelve poems of
outstanding quality, to add to the twenty he already had
available, for revision, from before 1857.

In preparing this new and greatly augmented edition (now
numbering some 127 poems in all), Baudelaire was not content merely to interpolate the new texts at various appropriate
points in the existing book; he seized the opportunity to
remodel its entire structure, in the light of his further creative
development. The most important change he made was the
addition of a whole new second section. 'Tableaux parisiens',
having as its nucleus eight poems which had figured already in the
'Spleen et Idéal' section of 1857. As to the other five sections
of the 1861 edition, the third, fourth and fifth of these ('Le
Vin', 'Fleurs du Mal' and 'Révolte') remain effectively unchanged as to their content (except for revisions of detail, of
course); their order, however, is significantly altered in the
following respects. The continuity between the last two 1857
sections, 'Le Vin' and 'La Mort', maintained in 1857 from
the 'representative' scheme of *Les Limbes*, is now finally
broken; 'Le Vin' loses its undue importance as the
penultimate section, and is made to follow 'Tableaux parisiens' and precede the other three. The penultimate place is
now assumed by 'Révolte' − a recognition of its logical connection with 'La Mort', derived from a shared religious context. As to the individual poems added in 1861, most of these
(19 out of 32) go to enlarge the first section, 'Spleen et Idéal',
and are accommodated without difficulty within its three love
'cycles' and other main groupings; the most important additions are those made to the 'Spleen' series, which now gains
strong reinforcement from the addition of *Obsession*, *Le
Goût du néant* ('The Taste for Nothingness'), *Alchimie de la*

douleur ('The Alchemist of Sorrows') and *Horreur sympathique* ('Self-reflections in a Stormy Sky'), with *L'Horloge* ('The Clock') as a newly dramatic finale replacing the pleasant but unexciting *Pipe* of 1857. The other section to benefit substantially from new additions is the final one, 'La Mort'; this is now transformed from the symmetrical 1857 series of three lightweight sonnets, into a powerful and many-sided exploration of the unknowable, with three further poems added, one of which, *Le Voyage* ('The Travellers'), is the longest that Baudelaire ever wrote.

The various changes as well as additions brought by Baudelaire to his second edition of *Les Fleurs du Mal* – which include also, as in 1857, appropriate transitions from one poem to another, in the case of each new interpolation – both explain and give renewed emphasis to what he wrote some ten months later, in mid-December 1861, to his friend and distinguished contemporary Alfred de Vigny:

The one compliment I would seek for this book is the recognition that it is not a mere album, and that it has a beginning and end. All the new poems have been written expressly to be adapted to the distinctive framework I have chosen.   (*CPl* II, p. 196)

'Not a mere album' because, as in 1857, the poems had been carefully grouped, and their presentation meticulously planned in their relation one to another; 'a beginning and an end', because the book opens, in *Bénédiction*, with the narration of a generic poet's birth, and closes, in *Le Voyage*, with the vision of a death (the Travellers') which yet promises *re*birth into the new. And when Baudelaire goes on, in his second sentence, to say that the new poems have been written expressly to be adapted to the 'distinctive framework' he has chosen, what he here has in mind, of course, is not some overall, collective 'message' supposedly conveyed by the book as a whole (this is the 'architectural' fallacy first propounded in 1857 by Barbey d'Aurevilly, though never by Baudelaire himself), but rather the careful groupings and sequences he is here modifying from the first edition – the most notable such modification being his addition of an entire further section (the 'Tableaux parisiens') in which he was able to include several of his finest newly composed poems.

Les Fleurs du Mal (1868)

The 1861 edition of *Les Fleurs du Mal* was not only the last that Baudelaire himself prepared, but also the last that Poulet-Malassis was, for legal reasons, able to publish. The remaining five years of Baudelaire's working life, till his crippling cerebral stroke in March 1866, were a sad tale of his repeated but unsuccessful attempts to find another publisher for the augmented third edition of his poems that he himself planned, and for which he held ready a special copy of the 1861 text, interleaved with such further editions as he was willing or able to sanction. Ironically enough when, in 1868, in the year following Baudelaire's death, the third edition of *Les Fleurs du Mal* did finally appear, it was under the imprint of Michel Lévy – the publisher since 1856 of Baudelaire's Poe translations, but also the intended original publisher of his poems under their first titles, *Les Lesbiennes* and *Les Limbes* . . .

It is really only by virtue of its comprehensiveness that this third edition of *Les Fleurs du Mal* merits serious consideration. It was the work of Baudelaire's friends, Banville and Asselineau (mainly the former), and was in effect a mere compilation of all the verse texts of Baudelaire's (apart from the 'pièces condamnées') which had been published during his lifetime and which were thought to be worth reprinting – with, as a single addition, the sonnet he had dedicated to . . . Banville in 1845. The text of the new edition certainly benefited from a few improvements here and there, but very little care seems to have been taken with the actual arrangement of the poems, on which Baudelaire had himself lavished such attention: thus of the 25 additional poems, 20 were simply tagged on, without any visible justification, to the end or towards the end of the first section, 'Spleen et Idéal', which was now therefore enlarged to even more massive proportions – from 77 poems out of 101 in 1857 and 85 out of 127 in 1861, to a still more unwieldy 107 out of 152 in 1868.

Chapter 2

Themes

Baudelaire and the French lyric tradition

The nineteenth century brought a second heyday of the French lyric tradition – the first having occurred three centuries earlier, in the Renaissance. It is in any case appropriate to date this tradition mainly from the sixteenth century, in view of the rapid development of printing at that time and the resulting wider circulation of texts.

Lyric poetry in the French Renaissance was mainly amorous in theme, and cast in the shorter forms (*dizain* or sonnet): Scève's *Délie*, Du Bellay's *L'Olive*, Ronsard's series of *canzoniere*, dedicated respectively to Cassandre, Marie and Hélène. But there were also, to take but a few further examples, the two collections inspired by Du Bellay's sojourn in Rome: the satirical and nostalgic *Regrets*, the elegiac meditations of *Les Antiquités de Rome*, or the closely argued spiritual cogitations of Sponde's *Sonnets de la mort*.

The next two centuries in France saw a decline in the quality as well as the quantity of lyric verse. Other genres, it is true, abound; as Margaret Gilman remarks (*The Idea of Poetry in France*, p. 6), in the eighteenth century 'odes, idylls, epigrams, fables, satires, didactic poems, all came off the poetic assembly line with appalling regularity' – whilst earlier, in the seventeenth century, the true primacy in verse had passed to the dramatists and especially to the incomparable Racine. At the end of the eighteenth century, however, appeared a genuine lyricist, Chénier; unpublished until 1819, he was then taken as a precursor by the poets of the new Romantic generation. For these: Lamartine, Hugo,

Vigny, the expression of personal emotion still tended to be couched in general terms linked with meditation on such great abstractions as 'Time', 'Nature', 'Solitude', 'Infinity' and the like; a more intimate vein was explored by Sainte-Beuve, Musset and the lesser Romantics, but Baudelaire remains the first to have developed a truly self-analytical mode, at once sharp and precise, while in his love poetry both returning to and renewing Renaissance models. To this extended lyricism of subject-matter he lends further emphasis by basing on it, as we have seen, the whole intricate if retrospective organisation of his book – and this is one reason why I have chosen to devote an entire chapter to the examination of certain of his themes. (Another reason, equally good, is that a poem's theme, developed over its whole length, needs to be examined separately from its detailed even though related elements.) I say 'certain' of Baudelaire's themes advisedly: we are not obliged, in thus surveying the subjects he treated, to follow slavishly the classification he himself adopted in his editions of 1857 and 1861. For one thing, it happened that, for circumstantial reasons, neither of these two editions could be fully comprehensive; for another, those themes which his own groupings brought into particular prominence, are not necessarily those which most interest us as modern readers, or best typify his originality as it has emerged in the perspective of time. A final point: in Baudelaire's verses as in anyone else's, themes tend to overlap from one poem to another, and in such cases we need to be free to consider these themes under more than one heading.

The love poet

In March 1846, at the outset of a dazzling set of 'Consoling Maxims on Love', the young Baudelaire addresses his readers thus: 'If I begin by speaking of love, it is because love is for everyone – deny it who may – the one great thing in life!' (*OCP* I, p. 546). Even at twenty-five, Baudelaire was here speaking from hindsight – not only as a promiscuous lover who had already contracted the venereal disease which was to dog him all his life, but as a writer who had by now composed nearly all the love poems which form by far the most substantial part (more than a third) of his verse output. In the most exact sense, therefore, love was indeed for him, and would continue to be, the 'one great thing in life': it dominated and undermined his day-to-day existence, it 'made' him as a poet and destroyed him, subtly, as a man. From the creative point of view, these love poems are his particular glory; as Henri Peyre pointed out many years ago (*Connaissance de Baudelaire*, p. 79), Baudelaire is here without rival among French poets – only Ronsard, 300 years previously, approaching him in his 'sovereignty as a lyricist of love'.

The simplest way of writing a love poem to a lady is to particularise, admiringly, her charms. This highly traditional form of tribute may be either comprehensive or selective: in the latter case it may, as in the *blasons anatomiques* of certain sixteenth-century French poets, be narrowed down to an obsessive fetishism. Or again, the tribute to the lady's physical beauties may be linked to the celebration (more frequently, the idealisation) of her moral qualities: the mode then becomes Petrarchan. All these variations on a theme which, in its truly formalised sense, dates only from the Renaissance, are to be found in Baudelaire's love poems – but adapted, and in some cases transformed, to fit the exigencies of a 'modern' lover: complex, sophisticated, self-doubting, often perverse.

Perhaps the most complete example of the genre is *Le Beau Navire* ('The Proud Ship'). Here, from the outset, Baudelaire declares his intention of describing the varied beauties of his mistress – neatly encapsulating, in his two opening lines, this whole traditional theme of fervent eulogy:

> Je veux te raconter, ô molle enchanteresse!
> Les diverses beautés qui parent ta jeunesse . . .

(Let me describe to you, o gentle enchantress, the diverse charms that adorn your youth . . .)

The catalogue of charms is here complete and exhaustive, as it equally is in such texts as *Le Serpent qui danse* ('Like a Serpent dancing'), *Chanson d'après-midi* ('Song for an Afternoon') and *Les Bijoux*; in this last poem, which earned 'condemnation' in 1857 but is perhaps the most remarkable and beautiful of them all, the entranced poet contemplates the woman lying before him in all the splendour of her nudity, as her jewels glitter and her dark skin glows in the firelight. So, too, in the third sonnet, *Le Cadre* ('The Picture Frame'), of the sequence *Un fantôme*, the naked Jeanne is recalled, over many years, as she once was in her heyday — artless, childlike, graceful, delighting in the enchanted 'separateness' which set her off from all that surrounded her, as if to contain and concentrate elements of beauty that might otherwise flow away and disperse. In *Tout entière* ('Total Harmony'), Baudelaire praises his lady's beauty by refusing, paradoxically, to describe it at all to the wily Satan, on the grounds that to itemise in any way would be to disrupt a harmony so exquisite that it resists analysis into its component 'chords'; each of the poet's senses, rather, is mysteriously fused into one: sound (the music of her voice) being apprehended as perfume, perfume (the fragrance of her breath) transmuted into sound. More particularised tributes celebrate the beloved's grace of carriage: *Avec ses vêtements ondoyants et nacrés* . . . ('In her shimmering, pearly garments . . .'), or the 'vertiginous prodigy' of her kisses: *Le Poison*; both these poems display, in their account of the poet's attitude to his beloved, an entirely modern ambivalence, and in this respect one of the most interesting of all Baudelaire's love poems, and one of the finest, is *Ciel brouillé* ('Troubled Sky'). The woman's charms here hold the same ambiguity as those of autumn; they are at once seductive and threatening — seductive in themselves, threatening because of Baudelaire's very uncertainty as to what lies ahead, as winter follows autumn and in her own case . . . who can tell?

In these and other similar poems of amorous tribute, an undoubted physical interplay between the two partners is implied; elsewhere, the pattern is more widely and fascinatingly varied. Thus Baudelaire wrote a certain number of more or less platonic love poems: in *Que diras-tu ce soir* . . ., *Le*

Flambeau vivant, *Hymne*, it is the beloved's effective moral influence that is eulogised, in a Petrarchan vein; in *L'Aube spirituelle* ('The Spiritual Dawn'), *Réversibilité*, *L'Irréparable*, the conviction or hope is expressed that she may somehow rescue him from the degradation into which he has fallen. I spoke earlier of ambivalence in the poet's attitude, and this we see most strongly in such poems as *Duellum* ('The Duel'), *Tu mettrais l'univers entier dans ta ruelle . . .* ('At your bedside you would welcome the whole universe . . .'), *Le Vampire*, *A une Madone*, and, most strikingly of all, the 'condemned' *A celle qui est trop gaie*; the last two of these poems elaborate sadistic fantasies, such as emerge also in *Madrigal triste* ('Sinister Gallantries') and the opening three stanzas (separable from the rest) of *L'Héautontimorouménos* ('The Self-Tormentor'). A further condemned poem offers the classic counterpart of sadism, in the fervently masochistic submission of *Le Léthé* – a mood perhaps glimpsed also, more obliquely, in the final lines of the later *Causerie* ('Conversation').

The poems so far mentioned (with the exception of *Le Cadre*) are all firmly located in the here and now. But it is a mark of Baudelaire's temperament – and in this he departs radically from lyrical tradition – that the past is often desired more strongly and vividly than the present. In the whole sequence *Un fantôme*, he poignantly recalls Jeanne as she was in her heyday, and in his memory still, defiantly, remains; in two further poems, that past still impinges on the present – in his poignant hope, in *Le Balcon* ('On the Balcony'), that its happiness may even yet, in spite of everything, be somehow revived in the present; in his perverse longing, in *Une nuit que j'étais près d'une affreuse Juive . . .* ('One night as I lay beside some hideous Jewess . . .'), for the absent beauty he by this very token has chosen to abjure. But Baudelaire's fixation with past love has its strangest expression of all in a haunting quatrain of the second *Fantôme* sonnet, *Le Parfum*: how deeply and magically intoxicating, he here explains to his reader, is the charm that the remembered past confers upon the present – allowing a lover to pluck, from an adored body, the exquisite flower of memory! But there is still another sense in which a love poem may become also – or indeed primarily – a poem of memory. In *Parfum exotique*, in *La Chevelure* ('Within her Tresses'), by implication also in *Mœsta et errabunda* ('The Sad and Wandering One'), poet and mistress are in the closest physical contact; yet in each poem, his thoughts wander luxuriantly (if a shade ungallantly?) *from* her to the exotic scenes which by the details of her person, or her own 'vagrant' longings, she recalls for him from his voyagings of 1841–2. Nor is the past the only amorous 'elsewhere' that the poet may long for, or seek to promote above the present: in the future, too, may lie the secret of true happiness – whether in life still (*L'Invitation au voyage*, 'Invitation to a Journey'; *Le Vin des amants*, 'The Lovers' Wine'), or in death only (*La Mort des amants*).

Within the more conventional context of the love lyric viewed over many centuries, Baudelaire composed several poems of 'gallant' type recording passing encounters ('gallant' being a word he did not disdain, applying it or allowing it to be applied to a whole section, 'Galanteries', of the *Epaves*, 'Relics', of 1866); some of these poems are only potentially erotic, others again are simply and respectfully admirative of feminine charm. Two highly beautiful poems of this type have a decidedly anecdotal content: *Confession*, in which Baudelaire displays his exceptional narrative gift, and *Le Jet d'eau* ('The Fountain'). More conventional still, at least in this respect, are four poems which ring the changes on a time-honoured *topos* that one might call 'The Poet's Revenge', and of which the prototype in France is that most celebrated of Ronsard's *Sonnets pour Hélène*: *Quand vous serez bien vieille, au soir, à la chandelle . . .* (in Yeats's translation: 'When you are old and grey and full of sleep . . .'). In Baudelaire's versions of this theme: *Remords posthume* ('Posthumous Remorse'); *Une charogne* ('The Carrion', in its last three stanzas); *Je te donne ces vers . . .* ('To you I dedicate these verses . . .'); *Le Flacon* ('The Perfumeflask'), he too is in effect repeating, half-scoldingly, to the woman he loves, what so many others have said before him:

'You may scorn me now, but take heed! If you are ever remembered in the future, it will be solely because of me, who have sung your praises in verses which will still be read long after the time when you, but for them, would be totally forgotten . . .'

I have reserved, until the last, four extraordinary love poems of a type that seems unique to Baudelaire: *Causerie*; *Sonnet d'automne* ('Sonnet for Autumnal Lovers'); *Semper eadem* ('Ever the Same'); *Chant d'automne* ('Song of Autumn' − in its second part only); collectively I would apply to these poems the title once given by Elizabeth Bowen to a novel of hers: *The Death of the Heart*. An anticipation of these texts is perhaps to be found already in line 8 of the sonnet *Duellum*, evoking the furious 'ulcerations' left by love in 'mature hearts'; as to the four 'Death of the Heart' poems, these extend over several years of the poet's life, but even in what is clearly the earliest of them, *Causerie* (of which there has recently been discovered a manuscript which I would date from the early 1850s), Baudelaire had already left far behind him the passions of youth. All four of these poems share a certain anecdotic framework, in that in each the lovers are glimpsed together in circumstances of great intimacy (in the very act of making love, indeed, in *Causerie*), but in which psychological relationships are as important as physical. In all four poems passionate love is presented as a threatening and destructive force which the poet has come to fear − but which, again in the first of the four, *Causerie*, he is not yet ready to flee entirely. It is true he here shows himself already all too well aware of the ravages love has wrought in him, and which he images in two astonishing fantasies of destructive violence; yet in the end he still surrenders to a force that in this context seems irresistible. 'Your hand laid on my breast' (he at first protests) 'seeks out my heart in vain − for that heart is a desert, laid waste by women's teeth and claws; wild beasts have devoured it utterly! It is a palace under siege, invaded by a mob of drunken, murderous vandals!' But he continues: 'And yet, and yet . . . I breathe in the perfume that swirls around your naked breasts: since it is your wish, scourge me then with your beauty! With your glittering eyes, in their festive brilliance, *consume* these tattered shreds that the beasts have disdained!'

In the remaining three poems of the group, a still further stage has been reached: the poet is now resigned to seek consolation in tenderness alone, in a gentle forgetfulness of the death which threatens and which cannot anyway be resisted. And yet, in one at least of these further poems, *Sonnet d'automne*, the memory is still sharp of those searing passions, of that 'dark legend written in fire', of the perennial Cupid now seen anew in a sinister refashioning of the traditional emblematic of Love: 'Cupid, stealthy and shadowy in his hiding-place, is waiting in readiness to draw his fatal bow. I know only too well the weapons in that age-old armoury of his: crime, horror and madness!' In modern parlance, that 'fatal bow' could be a Mauser or a sub-machine gun . . . And we recall that in a cognate poem with a more general theme, *L'Amour et le crâne* ('Cupid astride the Skull'), the God of love is again shown (or is seen by Baudelaire, in his re-interpretation of an old engraving) as an enemy rather than as a friend of Man, who at the end exclaims in outraged protest to his 'monstrous assassin': 'what your cruel mouth is scattering into the air, is torn from the very skull you so brazenly straddle – from my brain, from my blood, from my flesh!'

In these love poems taken as a whole, Baudelaire has probed with unparalleled insight and a new vividness and authenticity of language into the whole range of amorous experience: its delights and exaltations (in prospect and retrospect, as well as in actuality), its ambivalences and fantasies, its rancours and disillusions, its fears and consolations – entirely renewing for our times this most traditional of poetic genres.

The self-analyst

It is above all by the intensity of his self-analysis in *Les Fleurs du Mal* that Baudelaire differentiates himself from his predecessors – as may be seen from a whole series of poems in which (matching the equally precocious insight displayed in the novella of 1843–6, *La Fanfarlo*), he subjects his own thoughts, feelings, fantasies and behaviour to the most rigorous and unsparing scrutiny.

A first and obvious category of such poems is that identified by the initial word, 'Spleen', in the antithetic title, 'Spleen et Idéal', of the opening section of *Les Fleurs du Mal*. This term had been freely utilised as a synonym or variant (deemed characteristically English) of 'ennui', since at least the late 1820s, by such writers as Musset, Vigny, Gautier, Flaubert, Balzac and the minor Romantics Petrus Borel and Philothée O'Neddy. Baudelaire, however, when drafting his own poems of this type in the 1840s, seems to have preferred the French term, and to have replaced this by 'spleen' only around 1851, when he applied it as a title to three poems published in that year and in all to seven, though in 1857, finally, only to four, while incorporating it also in the title of the first section of his book. As the word's interchangeability with 'ennui' clearly shows, the initial and determining characteristic of 'spleen' is boredom; but its further ingredients (like those of Leopardi's *noia* – powerfully conveyed, earlier in the century, through very similar poetic images) include inertia, deep melancholy, a profound despair. There is also, literally or metaphorically, a climatic element, as we can plainly see from all four of the named *Spleen* poems, from *Brumes et pluies* ('Mists and Rain'), from *De profundis clamavi* ('Out of the Depths I called to Thee' – this opening line from the penitential psalm replacing, in 1857, the previous title *Le Spleen*): in all these poems it is the arrival of winter that sets off a corresponding mood, which in turn may be figured by imagery descriptive of that time of year. The most impressive and moving of all these 'splenetic' texts forms the first part of *Chant d'automne* – these four stanzas being eventually combined under that title, in 1859, with a further three expressly written for Marie Daubrun. In the opening lines of this first part, we see the poet alone, beleaguered in his room at the fall of the year, listening in alarm to a familiar sound that threatens from outside: the logs falling in the courtyard, as the carts ply their rounds discharging their store of firewood for the winter. And this sound, as well as stirring up a whole seasonal neurosis in him, made up of anger, hatred, cold horror, the prospect of forced and bitter toil, puts him in mind of other more sinister, specifically funereal sounds: a scaffold being built, a tower being brought down by a battering ram, a coffin being nailed together. But as yet, hearing that sound outside, he can speak only of 'departure', of winter succeeding to autumn, and cannot quite bring himself (as he does, finally, in the second half of the poem) to voice his underlying premonition of death.

Beyond the winter mood, still further depths of prostration, linked with feelings of guilt and negative emotions of all kinds, are evoked in *La Cloche fêlée* ('The Cracked Bell'), *Réversibilité*, *L'Irréparable*, *La Musique*. The finality of despair is reached in two very different poems: the early *Le Mort joyeux* ('Happier Dead'), to which also the title *Le Spleen* was at first given, and the altogether more powerful, indeed devastating, *Le Goût du néant*, published and no doubt composed in the aftermath of the trial of 1857. The very last flicker of energy has here been dispersed, in a total paralysis of all the poet's faculties − a paralysis epitomised in the poignant line: 'Le Printemps adorable a perdu son odeur!', which in its context carries the meaning 'Even the adorable spring has for me lost its fragrance!'.

All these 'spleen' poems are, for the most part, morally neutral, in that Baudelaire here abstains from passing judgment on the state of mind into which he has fallen. A more self-aware stance is adopted in several further poems, in which he records terrifying obsessions (*La Fontaine de sang*, 'The Fountain of Blood'; *Les Métamorphoses du vampire*; *Obsession*; *Le Gouffre*, 'The Abyss'), or avows with audacious frankness erotic or sadistic fantasies (*La Destruction* − in its tercets, a personal transposition of the two concluding stanzas of *Au Lecteur*). More comprehensive is the defiant, even arrogant confession of delinquency or sheer perversity in such poems as *Le Rebelle*, *Les Deux Bonnes Sœurs* ('The Two Sisters of Mercy'), the paired *Alchimie de la douleur* and *Horreur sympathique*, and, finest of all, *L'Ir-rémédiable* – that brilliant series of 'emblems' (Baudelaire's word) exemplifying in a series of claustrophobic tableaux the predicament of one condemned to an inescapable doom, yet able to 'console' himself ironically, at the end, with the clear knowledge, at least, of the sins he has committed: 'la con-science [consciousness, not conscience!] dans le Mal'. But irony, if at times salutary, may at others prove dire and crip-pling – as in *L'Avertisseur*, with its insufferable *warning* viper, ever prompt to negate the least stirring of desire or am-bition, or *L'Héautontimorouménos*, with the poet here con-fronting 'la vorace Ironie' as his own mirror-image.

Without self-irony the poet may, of course, as in *La Béatrice*, become merely the victim of the one he most loves, and the butt of those he most hates (personified in this in-stance as dwarf-like demons). He may also, as in *L'Examen de minuit* ('The Midnight Confession'), now bereft of dignity of any kind and on an ominous Friday the 13th, heap upon himself a scathing reminder of all the day's petty misdeeds and squalid meannesses. But the most savagely self-lacerating of all Baudelaire's poems, the most painful of all to read, is unquestionably *Un voyage à Cythère*. In this text, going back in its first version to 1844–5, the poet narrates his departure on a sea-voyage to the famed island of Venus, Cythera; as he draws alongside, however, what he sees is something far dif-ferent from the sighing hearts and warbling doves and ardent priestesses of legend: it is a hanged man on a gibbet, his corpse horribly assailed by ferocious birds and avid beasts, a lamentable figure with whom the poet instantly identifies – for has he not, too, been punished in his own flesh for the crimes of love he has committed? And thus, although at the poem's close the sky remains as cloudless, the sea as calm as ever, for him henceforth everything has become black and drenched with blood – with the two final lines intimating that it is above all the manifest symptoms of the venereal disease now disfiguring his own body and heart, that have prompted the poet to identify so closely with his brother-in-sin upon the gibbet:

>   – Ah! Seigneur! donnez-moi la force et le courage
> De contempler mon cœur et mon corps sans dégoût!   60

(Ah! Lord, give me strength, give me courage just to *look* on my own heart and body without disgust!)

Nowhere else in his poetry does Baudelaire speak thus personally to God; this final couplet of *Un voyage à Cythère* – first drafted perhaps on the very eve of his suicide attempt of 30 June 1845 – seems thereby all the more unbearably poignant in its bitter, anguished sincerity.

The practising poet

Incited to renew a stock Romantic theme by his personal experience in 1841–2 at the hands of his family, Baudelaire around that time composed a number of poems in which he deplored the generic Poet's or Artist's alienated, even persecuted place in society and defended, in the face of that alienation, his claim (in the Poet's or Artist's name, or his own) to pursue the ideal rather than the real and mundane: *L'Albatros*; *La Mort des artistes* ('The Death of Artists'); *Sur 'Le Tasse en prison' d'Eugène Delacroix* ('On Eugène Delacroix' Painting, *Tasso in Prison*'); *La Voix* ('The Preferred Voice'); *Les Plaintes d'un Icare* ('The Lament of an Icarus'); above all, *Bénédiction*, that passionately self-inspired chronicle of the Poet's victimisation on earth but 'benediction', or apotheosis, in Heaven. A more original view of the creative vocation, is offered in *Les Phares* ('The Beacons'), with its presentation of eight great artists of the past and present, their work brilliantly crystallised within eight single quatrains or 'medallions', as supreme witnesses to man's courageous, even challenging dignity before God.

Baudelaire also breaks new ground, this time in the pioneering exploration of his own creative experiences and problems as a poet, in a series of poems he placed together, near the beginning of his book, in 1857 as again (except in the first of these cases) in 1861: *Le Soleil* ('The Sun', lines 5–8); *La Muse malade* ('The Ailing Muse'); *La Muse vénale* ('The

Venal Muse'); *Le Guignon* ('The Jinx'); *Le Mauvais Moine*
('The Indolent Monk'); *L'Ennemi*. In the second and third of
these six 'poems about poems', Baudelaire ironically adapts
to his own case the Romantic convention of the poetic Muse;
the fourth, *Le Guignon*, curiously illustrates in its own composition the very creative problems with which Baudelaire
was faced: it is largely composed of skilfully welded borrow-
ings from Gray's *Elegy Written in a Country Churchyard* and
Longfellow's *A Psalm of Life*. As to the last two, *Le Mauvais
Moine* and *L'Ennemi*, these are particularly interesting in that
they paradoxically make a poem out of the very difficulty of
writing a poem; Baudelaire, who characterised his *alter ego*,
Samuel Cramer, at the very outset of *La Fanfarlo*, as 'le dieu
de l'impuissance', was certainly one of the first-ever poetic
analysts in France of the creative predicament later to be explored more fully by his successors Mallarmé and Valéry, and
in our own time to acquire the status of an accredited syn-
drome: 'writer's block'. *L'Ennemi*, the most accomplished
and moving of all the poems in this group, begins as a sort
of miniature narrative of the poet's creative life, picturing it
as a garden battered, in his earlier youth, by rains and storms
which have left few blooms still standing; as for the future,
who knows, now that the poet has reached the 'autumn of his
ideas' (which is not at all to be equated with the autumn of
his life, since Baudelaire was only thirty-four when he first
published, let alone drafted this poem), whether the 'new
flowers' of his dreams will find in that ravaged soil the
mysterious nourishment from which they could take root and
thrive? The final tercet, moving on to a more general plane,
identifies the 'enemy' of the title: what pain lies ahead for us
all, as Time eats away at our lives and we sense (bringing us
back to the obsessions of the self-analyst) some obscurely
hostile force feeding on our hearts and on the very blood that
ebbs away from us – growing strong as we grow weak, wax-
ing as we wane! Asselineau who, as Baudelaire's closest
friend and first biographer, knew him better than did anyone
else, declared in an article of 1857 that *L'Ennemi* held in itself
the book's whole 'key' and 'morality'. I take this to mean

that it is this poem above all others which confesses the inner secret of the whole arduous and painful creation of *Les Fleurs du Mal*.

The compassionate spokesman: victims and rebels

Though Baudelaire as a poet was far from being totally self-absorbed, his sympathies for his fellow-beings were decidedly selective. One sympathy he retained throughout his life, and not only during his brief phase (1848–51) of Republican/ Socialist activity, was for the underdogs of society – for its victims, its dispossessed, its outcasts, even its pariahs. In many of his poems, admittedly, this sympathy is expressed indirectly, as a by-product of the poet's recorded day-to-day urban experience; we may thus be sure that he himself had observed, with compassionate vigilance, the drunken, Napoleonic rag-picker of *Le Vin des chiffonniers* (and his analogue in lines 28-9 of *Les Litanies de Satan*, 'magically' preserved from the trampling horses into whose path he had strayed), the red-haired beggar-girl (fit for a palace!) of *A une mendiante rousse*, the pathetic yet heroic old ladies who tittup with dignity through *Les Petites Vieilles*. From a more distant personal experience may have come the inspiration for *A une Malabaraise*: the charming Malabar girl (or Indian girl, in the first published version, of 1846, of this poem) may well have been remembered by Baudelaire from his voyage of 1841 to the southern seas. More generally we find him imagining, for the humble folk of *La Mort des pauvres*, an after-life which will bring all those small worldly comforts which on earth have been denied them – or, again, in *Le Crépuscule du soir* ('Paris at Nightfall') and *L'Ame du vin* ('The Soul of Wine'), singling out for admiration the honest workman who toils doggedly and uncomplainingly in factory or field. This same (city) workman reappears in the final couplet of *Le Crépuscule du matin* ('Paris at Daybreak'), but is there more objectively presented, as a figure symbolising the whole renewed daytime activity of Paris after the grim and painful happenings of the night. Those grim happenings are in fact catalogued in both

Crépuscule poems, but with an interesting variation between the two (which perhaps has chronological significance) as regards the poet's approach and degree of commitment. Thus in *Le Crépuscule du matin*, the enumeration of events is made sensitively enough but dispassionately, without explicit comment of any kind; in *Le Crépuscule du soir*, on the other hand, the poem's second 'voice' (the first being altogether different in tone, as we shall see; pp. 32–3 and 41, below) records some of the same casualties of the night with a directly sympathetic involvement that rings out in the poem's final couplet:

> Encore la plupart n'ont-ils jamais connu
> La douceur du foyer et n'ont jamais vécu!   38

(How many indeed of these unfortunates have never known the comforts of home and hearth, and have never truly lived at all!)

A final poem within this explicitly 'compassionate' series, *Le Cygne* ('The Swan'), places the victims of society in the full forefront of the reader's attention; this is indeed, as we shall see in a later chapter, a poem for *all* such victims, at any time or anywhere.

It must not be thought that Baudelaire's championship of those existing on the margins of society is limited to the meek and inarticulate; it extends also, and more audaciously, to certain figures and groups who, far from accepting social condemnation and victimisation, defy it vigorously. Thus in *Don Juan aux enfers* (based on a contemporary lithograph), the philandering Don of legend remains for Baudelaire calmly disdainful and unrepentant to the very end (*L'Impénitent* was the title first given to this text, in 1846), as he is ferried away towards Hell. Still more aberrant, by conventional standards, is the Lesbian dissidence which held such particular fascination for Baudelaire, at least in his youth. The three poems here in question: *Lesbos*, and the two he ultimately entitled *Femmes damnées*, would in 1845–7 have constituted, at least in part, the eponymous first section of the projected *Lesbiennes* volume of that date; very probably, as I have argued elsewhere (*Baudelaire*, pp. 29–47), they would there have formed part of a verse novel set in classical times on the island of Lesbos, and celebrating and defending its reputed sexual rites. Baudelaire's viewpoint here is in its context highly unorthodox and original: the accepted conventional presentation of Sappho, for instance (e.g. in Lamartine's 'élégie antique' of that title), is of a chaste priestess of Venus who, in despair at being rebuffed by the boatman Phaon, throws herself from the Leucadian rock into the sea. What further distinguishes these three poems is not only their surpassing beauty of language and singular dramatic and narrative power, but also their elaboration of a whole counter-religion or counter-ethic, in which sin is ingeniously excused (indeed acclaimed) as a form of spiritual aspiration, an attempt to transcend the too-finite bounds established by convention; illicit desires thus become a symptom of Man's (or in this case, of Woman's) inner frustration and dissatisfaction with the here and now, and spirituality no longer remains the exclusive preserve of the virtuous. But this whole Lesbian counter-morality was to be comprehensively undermined in 1857, when at the end of his first *Femmes damnées* poem, Baudelaire decided, for prudential reasons, to add five stanzas in which, without prior warning, he thundered out a theological condemnation of Lesbian practices.

Even more than the Lesbian sisterhood, Baudelaire's group of religious rebels must be considered as outlaws within society – since against them is ranged the whole formidable establishment of the *bien-pensants*. It is often forgotten that Baudelaire in his youth, as several of his contemporary friends have testified, passed through a distinct atheistic or anti-religious phase; in *Les Fleurs du Mal* this is manifested above all in the 'Révolte' section proper, but it surfaces also, more incidentally, in a number of other verse texts – in *Le Rêve d'un curieux* ('A Curious Man's Dream'); in *Le Couvercle* ('The Lid'); in *Le Squelette laboureur* ('The Labouring Skeletons'); in *Le Jeu* ('The Gaming Table'); in *Les Aveugles* ('The Blind Men'). As for the three 'Révolte' poems – which, although each derives from a considerable Romantic tradition of anti-religion and Satanism, only narrowly escaped condemnation in the climate of 1857 – these are more varied in form, and less closely linked with one another, than are their counterparts in the Lesbian sequence. In the first poem, *Le Reniement de saint Pierre* ('St Peter's Denial of Christ'), Baudelaire boldly takes sides with St Peter, and therefore against a Christ who in the end meekly capitulated to a tyrannical God; a final stanza (perhaps added around 1849–51, as Claude Pichois, modifying Antoine Adam, has suggested) adds as a bitter personal comment the poet's dismissal of a world in which action – even violent action – is not married to dream. The second poem, *Abel et Caïn*, is no doubt the weakest of the three; its short-breathed apostrophes address respectively the progeny of the two brothers, in a series of vituperative or admonitory exclamations, which culminate in the command to the 'race de Caïn' to scale Heaven itself and cast down God. Altogether more felicitous is the final and in this case overtly blasphemous poem, *Les Litanies de Satan*, an audacious transposition or parody, in a long series of couplets, of the Litanies to the Virgin, punctuated by the unvarying refrain: 'O Satan, prends pitié de ma longue misère!' ('O Satan, take pity on the long misery I have endured!'). As these last words suggest, the supplication is made on behalf of all those whose sufferings entitle them to be placed under Satan's patronage and protection; they too are outcasts, like him, and in some way or other have earned the condemnation of society. A final 'Prayer', following the string of couplets, seems to envisage an ultimate triumph of Satan, in which the poet himself would hope to share. In the light of this text especially, one can appreciate just why Baudelaire should have felt it strategic (even though, as he admitted, 'detestable') to preface this whole section in 1857 with a note expressly contradicting in advance any such apparent personal application.

The poet as moralist

Whatever Baudelaire's sense of identification may have been

with the victims and rebels of this world, in other contexts he is more prone to adopt the judgmental standpoint of the moralist — whether in the French sense of the word (a critic of social custom and behaviour, of *mœurs*, in the seventeenth-century tradition of La Bruyère and La Rochefoucauld), or the English (a moraliser, tending towards didacticism). The purely didactic poems, carrying censorious recommendations for improved conduct, are not to modern taste — nor must they have been, in retrospect, to that of Baudelaire, since he included only three of them in the *Fleurs du Mal* of 1857, having by then come to endorse (*OCP* II, p. 333) Poe's denunciation of the 'Heresy of the Didactic'. The poems in question are *Les Hiboux* (the best of the three, but also the most explicit: from the owls in their stillness, the wise man should learn the folly of heedless movement hither and thither); *Le Châtiment de l'orgueil* (the moral lies solely in the title: the pride here punished is that of the vainglorious theologian reduced in an instant to imbecility); *Le Tonneau de la Haine* (the moral is stated through allegory: like a leaking cask which demands continually to be filled and refilled, Hatred can never be assuaged). Two further didactic poems were excluded by Baudelaire from *Les Fleurs du Mal*, but found their way into the posthumous edition of 1868: *La Rancon* (to gain the ultimate ransom of our souls in Heaven, we must labour long and arduously in the two fields of Charity and Art); *A une Malabaraise* (the Malabar girl is gently rebuked, in a discursive poem of considerable charm, for seeking to leave her native paradise for inimical, fog-bound Paris).

Much more incisive and commanding are the texts which, while denouncing or deploring this or that aspect of human behaviour, abstain from recommending alternative conduct for its improvement. In *Le Crépuscule du soir*, the first of two alternating 'voices' announces sardonically, at the outset, the arrival of yet another Parisian nightfall. The other 'voice' in the poem, heard immediately afterwards and as if in counterpoint, is a differently compassionate one — recording, rather, the solace and refreshment after toil that evening brings. But soon the sardonic voice, the *moralist's* voice, takes over

again, and for a further eighteen lines catalogu
sidious ramifications of Parisian vice and crim
catalogue echoed more briefly and generally,
later, within two further poems making the same l
sion: *Les Aveugles*, lines 10–12; *Recueillement*, 'N   ,
lines 5–7. Another suspect compulsion, that of gambling
(briefly referred to in *Le Crépuscule du soir*), is portrayed
with Balzacian vividness and vicarious envy in *Le Jeu*. More
strident altogether are the five stanzas, splendidly rhetorical
if rather cravenly conventional in spirit, added in 1857 as a
last-minute, precautionary condemnation of the Lesbian
couple, Delphine and Hippolyte, in the first *Femmes damnées*
poem. In *Le Couvercle*, what is more contemptuously
deplored by Baudelaire is Man's superstitious fear of an
unknown which is in fact no more than the *lid* of the stewpot
within which he and his fellows impotently simmer. In *Au
Lecteur*, each one of us stands accused of every imaginable
sin; this hectoring series of quatrains, with which Baudelaire
bludgeons his reader at the opening of his book, at least finds
a more felicitous ending – a sly *tu quoque* reminding us of
our joint complicity with him in that most heinous of all
vices, *ennui*:

> Tu le connais, lecteur, ce monstre délicat,
> – Hypocrite lecteur, – mon semblable, – mon frère!   40

(You know him only too well, that suavely refined monster – you,
hypocritical reader, brother of mine in sin!)

Baudelaire similarly associates his reader with himself, under
a generalised 'nous', in the powerful poem which becomes in
1861 the new ending to the first, 'Spleen et Idéal' section of
his book. This is *L'Horloge*, in which the voice speaking to
us almost throughout is the hideous, grating, insect-like whisper
of the *clock*, never failing to remind us, in every language
known to Man, that with each swiftly passing moment pain
will strike and pleasures flee – that since Time is an inveterate gambler who wins without ever needing to cheat, the
hour will soon enough come for all of us when everything we

might hope to call on: Luck, Virtue, Remorse, will have one thing only to say to us: die, miserable coward! now it is too late!

In the last period of his working life, between 1858 and 1863, Baudelaire wrote (or completed) three poems: *Danse macabre*, *Le Voyage*, *L'Imprévu* ('The Unforeseen'), which represent something of a new departure, in that he does here seem to have succeeded in acclimatising moral themes to modern anti-didactic tastes. One fresh advantage that he has gained lies simply in the greater *length* of these poems: within this larger framework, he can now give to his moral judgments their appropriate universal (and even, in *Danse macabre*, apocalyptic) context, and can now illustrate and diversify these judgments by displaying a rich diversity of human activities and types. His starting-point in *Danse macabre* is a statuette by Ernest Christophe, representing a skeleton elaborately gowned as if for a ball; Baudelaire's enraptured description of this figurine reflects his bizarre taste for what he calls 'l'élégance sans nom de l'humaine armature' ('the nameless elegance of the human frame'). Rationalising, so as to speak, from this eccentricity, the moralist in him whirls his skeleton, in imagination, into a Parisian ballroom thronged with dancers each having the smell of death upon him, yet each oblivious of the great ironic truth ('le train de ce monde conduit par la Mort' — 'the busy round of life as conducted by Death', as Baudelaire himself put it, *CPl* I, p. 547) enshrined in the mediaeval concept of the 'branle universel de la danse macabre' ('the universal gyrations of the dance of death'). But it would seem that 'universal' here has an unexpected range, in time as well as space: this pungent modernisation of the *danse macabre* expands by the poem's close to a vision of 'risible Humanity', the whole world over, madly gallivanting its way towards final judgment. *Le Voyage* significantly takes up the theme which Baudelaire had already treated didactically in *Les Hiboux*, as well as in some discarded closing lines in the first version of 1846 of *A une Malabaraise*: that of the folly of needless movement from one place to another. Baudelaire's world-weary travellers, in sections IV and VI of *Le Voyage*, are similarly scathing about the futility of travel and the universality of sin it discloses; but the seventh and penultimate section brings a rather different and more ambivalent answer: 'Should one depart, should one stay? Stay, if you can; go, if you must. One person may rush to flee, another may crouch in hiding, both seeking to elude the vigilant, deadly enemy, Time!' The last in date of these three poems, *L'Imprévu*, brings a certain attenuation of the rigours of Baudelaire's misanthropy: whereas in most of these 'moralist' poems, the flagrancy of human sin or folly is untempered by any prospect of salvation, here, in this most orthodox of his poems from the theological standpoint (we are a long way, now, in spirit as well as time, from the 'Révolte' sequence of the 1840s!), we are offered a final consoling message by those who have accepted God's gift of suffering on earth. The poem opens, however, with a series of tiny, satirical vignettes, or thumbnail sketches, in which four of Satan's predestined victims as it were condemn themselves out of their own mouths; the clock meanwhile, as in *L'Horloge*, ticks away insidiously its unheeded message of Man's ripeness for damnation. Then Satan arrives to claim, and surprise, his prey – and this is the 'unforeseen' event of which the poem's title forewarns. But the poem has a double unexpectedness, for upon Satan's harangue there breaks in, antiphonally, the sound of the Angel's trumpet calling the blessed to their felicity, as the celestial harvests are gathered in.

Baudelaire has clearly moved far, in these three poems, from the direct and particularised didacticism of his earlier years; yet for all the strenuous denials of his letter to Swinburne of 10 October 1863 (*CPl* II, p. 325), he remains very much more of a moralist than he is prepared to admit, or than his mature aesthetic allows, as formulated in certain articles of 1857 and 1861 on fellow-writers. In these he disdains all explicit indictments (*OCP* II, pp. 81–2; cf. p. 333), claiming rather that it should be left entirely to the reader to draw his own moral from the 'natural lyrical development' of the writer's art (*OCP* II, pp. 186, 175), and praising Hugo for being, in certain shorter poems, a 'moraliste sans le vouloir' (*OCP* II, pp. 136–7). Baudelaire himself could certainly never be called an 'unwitting' moralist – rather an inveterate if increasingly subtle one.

The poet of Nature (and anti-Nature)

In the traditional sense of the phrase, Baudelaire could hardly be called a Nature-poet. As I have commented elsewhere (*Baudelaire and Nature*, pp. 317–18), he lacks almost entirely the exalted Nature-mysticism of a Wordsworth or a Lamartine, and Nature-description itself is virtually absent from his poetry. Indeed, there is one example only in the whole of *Les Fleurs du Mal*: the haunting *La Vie antérieure* ('A Former Life'), of the type of poem in which a specific landscape, or in this case seascape, is fixed for us in its distinctive physical detail, and in which the poet's subsequent emotional or philosophical response proceeds directly from the antecedent word-painting. Where Nature does feature in Baudelaire's poetry, it is almost always in its more general and elemental aspects; more often than not, moreover, the natural scene is evoked for some ulterior imaginative purpose – as an 'elsewhere', an antithesis to immediate reality (*Parfum exotique*; *La Chevelure*; *Mœsta et errabunda*; *L'Invitation au voyage*; the tercets of *Recueillement*), or as a symbol or 'correspondence' for personal moods or ideas (*De profundis clamavi*; *Ciel brouillé*; *Horreur sympathique*; *Avec ses vêtements ondoyants et nacrés* . . . , lines 5–8). There remain nevertheless, in addition to *La Vie antérieure*, some eight specific texts, of which the first seven will most probably have been composed in the 1840s, in which Nature does figure as a primary theme even if not descriptively.

The most influential of these poems is undoubtedly the sonnet *Correspondances*. This expresses a highly generalised and humanised view of Nature: as Man wanders through its vast temple, he finds himself bombarded by confusing messages which as it were challenge him to organize them into a coherent interpretation. The key to such an interpretation lies (in the second quatrain) in his varied sensory responses to what he perceives: from these diverse impressions coming together in his mind from so many quarters, a single *corresponding* and transcending unity can be inferred: 'Les parfums, les couleurs et les sons se répondent' ('Scents, colours and sounds give answer to one another'). The tercets privilege this general message in terms of one human sense alone, that of smell — taking as examples scents that can be understood in terms of touch (the flesh of children), of sound (the timbre of oboes), of colour (the green of meadows), or citing specific perfumes (amber, musk, benjamin, incense) that transport us into a world of infinitely expansive emotions: rich, triumphant, corrupt. A still more beautiful poem, *Harmonie du soir* ('Evening Harmonies'), pursues this same notion even further, but in the context of a personal response to a particular but not localised scene, centred no doubt in a garden. (So this is very much a townsman's view of Nature.) With extraordinary virtuosity (see p. 60, below), Baudelaire weaves together in a heady, swirling waltz the sounds and scents of the evening: 'Les sons et les parfums tournent dans l'air du soir'. But in this *valse triste* languor and sadness, expressed through imagery borrowed from the Catholic liturgy, pervade the scene; its horizons expand to take in the overarching sky and the sun sinking to rest in its clotted blood, and the complex of emotions is finally pierced by thoughts of the past and of a distant loved one: 'Ton souvenir en moi luit comme un ostensoir!' ('Your memory shines in me like a monstrance!')

In the first part of *J'aime le souvenir de ces époques nues* . . . , Baudelaire thinks back with regret, as the opening line indicates, to a Golden Age in which men and women, in the frank enjoyment of their nakedness, profited also from the favours of a benign natural environment. Now, alas! things are sadly different, and the continuity with Nature has been entirely lost: bodies are swaddled in infancy and further distorted by clothes thereafter, faces are ravaged by sin and debauchery — but this last development (the argument is not altogether coherent) does nurture a certain 'beauty of languor', and besides we have not yet lost our capacity to salute the freshness still preserved by youth. *L'Homme et la mer* elaborates, rather artificially, various analogies between Man and the sea: since the two share a common secretiveness and inner 'depth', a common love of carnage and death, Baudelaire wonders (why?) at the perennial and paradoxical hostility between them. The 'landscape' of *Paysage* is initially a winter *town*scape, which explains why Baudelaire grouped it in 1861 at the beginning of his 'Tableaux parisiens'; but what, from his garret and as an act of will, the poet chooses rather to conjure up instead, is a vision of springtime pastoral scenes, whereby to banish urban reality and strife. Finally, among these earlier Nature-poems of Baudelaire's, must be mentioned two youthful and conventional hymns to deities of Nature: *Le Soleil* and *Tristesses de la lune* ('A Melancholy Moon') – poems of the very type which in an open letter to Fernand Desnoyers, part-editor of the largely pastoral anthology of 1855, *Fontainebleau*, Baudelaire had declared himself quite unable to contribute . . .

That open letter (*OCP* I, pp. 1024–5), with its decisive repudiation of Nature, its rejection of the new and 'shocking' religion of Pantheism (Baudelaire uses the English adjective), and its explanation of his preferred decision to submit, instead, his two wholly Parisian *Crépuscules*, reflects a clear development in his Nature-philosophy. Already in two quatrains of *A celle qui est trop gaie*, he had expressed hostility to Nature – raging, by his 'punishment' of a flower, against what he sees as Nature's 'insolence', with its flagrantly unheeding ebullience mocking his own inertia; the context there being (perversely) amorous, the two quatrains lead on by analogy to a fantasied and explicitly sadistic attack on the poem's 'too joyous' dedicatee. He returns more comprehensively to the attack in 1859–61, in a whole section, 'Eloge du maquillage', of *Le Peintre de la vie moderne*, praising artifice and especially feminine make-up precisely for their salutary correction of the natural. An added poem, in the *Fleurs du Mal* of 1861, harmonises fully with this new thinking of Baudelaire's: this is the profoundly nihilistic sonnet *Obsession*, in which a deep-rooted 'hatred' for certain objects of Nature is prompted not by its indifference towards Man but rather by the too insistent *reminders* it brings of the poet's imprisoning self-image. Thus in the organ-like roaring of its forests he hears an echo of human sorrows; in the sound and swell of the ocean and its huge and ironic laughter, he detects his own vanquished likeness; as to the night sky, its stars speak a language known only too well to one whose need, rather, is for total emptiness, nakedness, darkness. But what then? – even onto the blackest night his mind persists in projecting images of departed friends, whose 'familiar glances' (so different from those welcome 'regards familiers' encountered, in *Correspondances*, in the temple of Nature!) he has now come to dread. The 'obsession' of the title, by which the poet feels himself so relentlessly pursued, lies in his helpless inability to escape, in Nature or indeed in anything else, the all-pervasive imprint of self.

The poet of Paris

Already as far back as 1852 (*CPl* I, p. 191), Baudelaire had shown his awareness of the distinctively Parisian character of certain of his writings, and we have seen how this led him, in 1861, to add to *Les Fleurs du Mal* – partly from poems already written, partly from others more recently composed or completed – a whole new section under the title 'Tableaux parisiens'. A further factor here was his pursuit of two parallel creative activities during this same period: his composition, firstly, of some at least of the prose poems to which in 1864 he was to give the collective title *Le Spleen de Paris*, and, secondly, of the essay *Le Peintre de la vie moderne*, devoted to an artist, Constantin Guys, whose 'modernity' lay at least partly in his brilliant evocation of Parisian society.

The title 'Tableaux parisiens' implies of course that the scenes depicted are *in* rather than *of* Paris – which is in fact the primary subject in three only of the poems: the two *Crépuscules* and *Le Cygne*. In all the others the city forms no more than a background – albeit, in nine of the cases, an important, even determining background: *Paysage*, 'Land-scape'; *Le Soleil*; *Les Sept Vieillards*, 'The Seven Old Men'; *Les Petites Vieilles*, 'The Little Old Ladies'; *A une passante*, 'To a Fair Passer-by'; *Le Jeu*; *Je n'ai pas oublié, voisine de la ville* . . . , 'I have not forgotten, near to the city, the little white house we lived in . . .'; *La servante au grand cœur* . . . , 'That great-hearted servant-woman of ours . . .'; *Rêve parisien*, 'A Parisian's Dream'. In the remaining six poems, however, the urban context is in truth no more than an incidental element — so that these poems might just as well have been transferred to some quite separate section, had Baudelaire not wished, in 1861, to fill out his Parisian con-tribution and emphasise particularly this aspect of his art.

Le Crépuscule du matin, although one of Baudelaire's earliest compositions and therefore metrically and stylistically unadventurous compared with such later poems as *Le Cygne*, still seems to me unrivalled in any language or medium as the complete evocation of the great modern city in which the con-centration of human distress and heartbreak is at its most devastating. In the brief opening section of this retrospective *tableau*, two distinct 'time signals' mark and fix the arrival of dawn: the bugle sounding reveille from the barracks, the fresh wind springing up to blow against the street lamps. And now, with dawn, comes that disquieting hour (memorably evoked in the poem's next section) when stress and conflict are at their greatest, when night struggles with day, lamplight with daylight, body with spirit; when adolescents are racked by disturbing dreams; when over everything is a sense of moral crisis and unease, of weariness and satiety, for man as for woman, in the labours of writing as in those of love, a sense above all of transience and aftermath, of things swiftly vanishing away — this last feeling hauntingly captured in the image of the tear-stained face drying in the wind. The ensuing third section fills in, objectively and almost flatly, the human and urban details of the scene. We see the first smoke rising from the chimneys, the chill mist swirling round the buildings, the sleeping prostitutes lying open-mouthed in their stupor, the spent debauchees trudging their way homewards, the numbed beggar-women, the mothers labouring in childbirth; we hear the cries of these same mothers, the piercing cock-crow, the last painful rattles in the throats of the dying. A final section of four lines rounds off this grim and unsparing picture with a last, cinematic 'long shot': Dawn, prettily personified in her pink and green frock, shivers her way down to the river, as waking Paris struggles reluctantly to life in the guise of an old workman reaching for his tools and shuffling off to begin his day's work. Daybreak in Paris is a time of sad endings, but also of painful beginnings: life goes on.

Le Crépuscule du soir is less uniform and concentrated in its mood than its companion poem and near-namesake; in this respect it approaches more closely to *Le Cygne* (to be studied in a later chapter), and it has, over and above its superficial discontinuity, a deep and grave consistency of tone which matches that of the later poem. I have mentioned already the two 'voices' which are heard alternately throughout the poem. The first is a sardonic voice, describing the realities of urban vice in a vivid but detached, almost amused manner: as night, the criminal's accomplice, steals stealthily upon the scene, impatient Man reveals himself as a wild beast. Prostitutes, thieves, gamblers roam the town and seem to take it over entirely; the air is filled with animal noises from theatres, concert-halls and restaurants; the city's turbulent activities mount a continued assault on the reader's sensibilities. But the second 'voice', which is no doubt more intimately the poet's own, is concerned with a quite different and more deeply serious aspect of this time of day. To some, to those who have worked hard and suffered long, evening brings solace and rest; to others, alas! it brings only illness, physical pain and death, an end to all the sweetness of life, if indeed that sweetness has ever been tasted at all.

To these three wholly Parisian poems (the two *Crépuscules* and *Le Cygne*) could be added three more which Baudelaire was unable, through circumstance, to place in the 'Tableaux parisiens' section of 1861. The first of these is the beautiful sonnet *Recueillement*, which was ready for publication only towards the end of 1861. The poet, at evening, has climbed to some high vantage-point above the city; beside him is his imagined 'companion', his Suffering, who has craved from him this benison of darkness. Spread out beneath them is the resting or careworn city, with its 'vile multitude' driven on by the scourge of Pleasure, launching itself upon a hectic nocturnal round that is no more than a laying-up (on earth) of future remorse. But the two turn away together from the Parisian scene, at the poet's gentle insistence, towards the west and the consoling spectacle of the clouds at sunset. A similar 'panoramic' view of the city forms, finally, the setting for an Epilogue Baudelaire had planned, but left uncompleted, for his second edition of 1861 of *Les Fleurs du Mal*; in this still somewhat perfunctory series of three-line stanzas, as equally in a second and longer draft Epilogue of more ambitious scope, Baudelaire shows more indulgence than in the two *Crépuscules* and in *Recueillement*, towards the capital's incredible human variety as well as depravity.

The great city of Paris, already in Baudelaire's day, was far from being a new topic for verse – as may readily be seen from Pierre Citron's compendious two-volume study of *La Poésie de Paris*; Baudelaire, however, elevates this theme above the merely topographical or polemical or frivolous (pastoral settings having been until then deemed more appropriate for serious poetry), dramatises the human destinies he sees played out against this complex background, above all displays his sympathetic curiosity for the extraordinary range of often mysterious behaviour he finds there.

The *transposition d'art* and the art of transposition

In the opening chapter to the *Salon de 1846*, while affirming the importance of the critic's personal reaction to a painting, Baudelaire suggests that the best way to review a picture might be to write a sonnet or an elegy about it (*OCP* II, p. 418). What Baudelaire does not here reveal – but what his friends at the time will have known well enough – is that he himself had already composed a considerable number of poems of this type (some nine in all), in which the subject is specifically a work of art. Baudelaire was by no means the inventor of this genre, which in its theoretical basis may be related to Horace's dictum 'Ut pictura poesis' ('As in painting, so in poetry', as David Scott renders it, *Pictorialist Poetics*, p. 5), and to later discussions − by Lessing in his *Laocoon*, for instance − of the affinity between the two arts; the most assiduous nineteenth-century practitioner in this field was Baudelaire's admired friend and colleague, Théophile Gautier − who, precisely between 1841 and 1844, published a number of poems on Spanish paintings and sculptures, which in 1845 were collected in book form under the title *España*, and to whom, some time later, we owe the useful descriptive term for such poems, *transposition d'art*.

Baudelaire's eleven poems on works of art (the nine composed in his youth, together with two more dating from 1858–9 and devoted to sculptures by Christophe) were never presented by him as a group in either of his two editions of *Les Fleurs du Mal*, but were dispersed throughout the volume according to their separate themes; indeed, Baudelaire rarely chooses to avow directly at all the 'plastic sources' of such poems, whatever may have been the contrary implication of the passage in the *Salon de 1846*. If, however, we do survey these poems together, as being demonstrably of a kind, we can discern an interesting variation, even gradation in Baudelaire's creative attitude and technique. Thus in five of the eleven poems, he begins with a more or less accurate description of the work of art in question. In *Une gravure fantastique*, this is an engraving, *Death on a Pale Horse*, after the eighteenth-century English artist, Mortimer (named only in the first published version, of November 1857), depicting dramatically the Fourth Horseman of the Apocalypse; in *Sur 'Le Tasse en Prison' d'Eugène Delacroix*, a painting, *Tasso in Prison*, by the French master ultimately designated in the title (albeit not in Baudelaire's original manuscript); in *Don Juan aux enfers* ('Don Juan in the Underworld'), a lithograph published in 1841 by one Simon Guérin (unnamed by Baudelaire); in *Bohémiens en voyage* ('Gypsies on the March'), an engraving by Callot (again unmentioned), from the sequence of four devoted to gypsies, *Les Bohémiens*; in *L'Amour et le crâne*, one of two engravings by Goltzius bearing the title 'Quis evadet?' ('Who can escape?'), but referred to by Baudelaire only in the most general terms, in his subtitles of 1855 ('After an old engraving') and 1857/1861 ('Tailpiece in an old book'). What we are finally given in each of these cases, however, when we reach the end of the poem, is Baudelaire's personal interpretation of the work in question – an interpretation that may on occasion run quite counter to the artist's declared intention, as in the case of *L'Amour et le crâne*, where Baudelaire converts Goltzius's reminder of the swift inescapability of Death, into an assertion of the implacable tyranny of Love over Man.

As it happens, in the most successful of all the five poems in this first group, *Don Juan aux enfers*, Baudelaire modifies not only the implicit intention but even the descriptive detail of the original – or rather, of what we *suppose* the original to have been, since no copy of it has been rediscovered since its first appearance in 1841, and we know it therefore only from a detailed contemporary prose description. Guérin, it would seem (the author of the lithograph), had chosen the Commander to be the dominant figure in his group – immobile and menacing in the prow of the boat in which Don Juan is being ferried off towards Hell. Behind the Commander, Guérin had placed the miscreant himself, haggard and remorseful, while all around him were grouped various of his desolate victims: Donna Anna, Donna Elvira, Zerlina, as well as others unnamed in the prose description of 1841. In Baudelaire's version (first published in 1846), the female victims are retained, but are effectively generalised into a wailing, writhing herd, half-naked in their distress; only the 'lean and chaste Elvira' is specifically identified, together with two other vividly characterised figures: the trembling, outraged Don Luis, the laughing, incorrigible Sganarelle. The Commander is still there, as impressive as ever at the helm; but it is Don Juan who has now, in the final couplet, become the dominant figure of all – studiedly disdaining his accusers as he leans elegantly upon his rapier, his eyes fixed only on the boat's wake as it glides away from our view. The Don, of course, as we have seen already, is a *rebel*, and as such commands the automatic admiration of the (rebellious) young Baudelaire – who, incidentally, made his admiration even more explicit in the poem's original title of 1846, *L'Impénitent*, which from the outset declares its 'calm hero' (Baudelaire's words) to be unrepentant, unashamed, to the very end. (By 1857 the poet could safely assume that no reader would still remember the lithograph of 1841, and could thus appropriate for himself the title *Don Juan aux enfers*, which Guérin had earlier been the first to choose.)

In a second group of these poems, Baudelaire adopts a more impressionistic approach, drawing not merely on one but on several plastic models. In *L'Idéal*, the theme is Baudelaire's *feminine* ideal, as captured in art – though not, certainly, in the derided vignettes of the day, nor in Gavarni's 'twittering flock' of etiolated 'hospital beauties'; what Baudelaire favours, rather, is the strong and powerful Lady Macbeth (for whom the admired model was no doubt one of Delacroix' illustrations to Shakespeare, rather than the original English text), or, again, Michelangelo's massive Florentine statue of Night. It is also in this second group that we find the most original and innovative of all Baudelaire's 'transpositions', *Les Phares*. Here he has singled out as shining *beacons* of human achievement eight great artists: Rubens, Leonardo da Vinci, Rembrandt, Michelangelo, Puget, Watteau, Goya, Delacroix, masterfully evoked in successive quatrains through a varying collage which on the one hand intermingles reminiscences of particular works (Leonardo's *Mona Lisa*, *Virgin of the Rocks*, *Virgin and Child with St Anne*; Michelangelo's *Last Judgment* fresco in the Sistine Chapel; Rembrandt's etchings, *Christ the Healer*, or *The Hundred Guilder Print*, and *The Three Crosses*; several engravings from Goya's *Caprichos* series) – and on the other, in the quatrains on Rubens, Puget, Watteau and Delacroix, gives a sort of composite impression of the artist's whole *œuvre*, drawn from elements common to several individual pictures or sculptures. The poem is rounded off by three further stanzas, which as it were reverberate endlessly upwards all those multiple curses, lamentations and ecstasies that together testify to Man's unquenchable dignity before God.

In Baudelaire's final group of poems about works of art, he takes us farther still from his starting-point, which here becomes in the end a mere pretext for a moral or philosophic excursion. Not that such a destination precludes an initial closeness of description: in each of the two Christophe poems of 1858–9, the whole first section is devoted to a detailed (and delighted) enumeration of particulars, the better to place the admired sculptures before the reader's eye. But thereafter, a wider theme emerges – especially in *Danse macabre*, as we have seen (p. 34, above), but also in *Le Masque*, in which the false face or 'mask', alone visible at first above the voluptuous body, turns out to conceal a true face contorted by grief; in the poet's interpretation, such grief alone is the valid reaction for all of us to a life that, somehow or other, we must contrive to go on living. Unlike *Danse macabre*, this is not one of Baudelaire's most successful poems – the reader being assailed from the very outset by a rhetoric that is at once stilted, grandiloquent and exhaustingly exclamatory.

Two further poems in this group complete Baudelaire's series of transpositions. The first, *Le Mauvais Moine*, is more laboured even than *Le Masque*; a line such as 'En ces temps où du Christ florissaient les semailles' ('In those times when Christ's teachings were fruitfully scattered abroad'), reminds us that even Baudelaire's apparently impeccable ear could on occasion fail to strike out a memorable and fluent rhythm; the 'plastic' reference to the fresco in the Campo Santo in Pisa, *The Triumph of Death*, then thought to be the work of Orcagna (directly named in the first, manuscript text), is in any case merely incidental to the poem's main theme. Altogether more successful is the swift octosyllabic evocation, in *Le Squelette laboureur*, of those gaunt figures stripped of flesh 'labouring' away in the pages of old anatomy books (Baudelaire is here no doubt thinking of one such book in particular, by Vesalius), to the terror of the poet seized by a premonition of endless continuing toil even after the promised nothingness of eternal sleep.

These eleven poems, with their new emphasis on the personal interpretation as well as the description of the model, clearly have an important place in the history of the *transposition d'art*; to the student of Baudelaire, they have added interest in that they show the mutual cross-fertilisation of two of his three main talents — the poet profiting from the knowledge as well as the intuition and sensibility of the art critic, the art critic happy to exploit the freedom of a totally imaginative and 'poetic' response to an admired painting or sculpture. (Baudelaire's third skill, the sole one recognised in his lifetime, was as a translator of Edgar Allan Poe.) But in the last resort, the poems must stand or fall by their aesthetic merit; by this criterion Baudelaire has, I suggest, succeeded brilliantly in five out of the eleven of these transpositions from one medium to another: in *Les Phares*, in *Don Juan aux enfers*, in *Le Squelette laboureur*, in *Danse macabre* and in *L'Amour et le crâne* — a considerable enough achievement, worthy to be measured against that of Gautier, in a difficult and ungrateful genre.

A punning title

I have left until the last any discussion of the title of Baudelaire's book — since this title, put forward at the end of 1854 by his friend Hippolyte Babou, will have been added long after the actual composition of all the poems contained in the *Fleurs du Mal* of 1857. But having gratefully appropriated Babou's inspired suggestion (no doubt seeing in it just that 'explosive' quality he so favoured in titles; see *CPl* I, p. 378), Baudelaire quickly invested it with his own meaning, and from analysing this we may gain an instructive insight into the retrospective view he took of his poems after 1854, both individually and as a collection.

In a letter to his publisher, Poulet-Malassis, written on 16 or 17 March 1857, Baudelaire opines as follows regarding the typographical presentation of his title: 'I think it would be a good idea to have *Fleurs* in italics — in slanting capitals, since it is a punning title' (*CPl* I, p. 382). A punning title ('un titrecalembour'): Baudelaire does not explain exactly where for him the pun lies, but obviously this relates to 'Fleurs' rather than 'Mal', since it is the former word that he suggests should be italicised. It is true that 'Mal', equally and more obviously, carries two meanings, since it may denote 'illness' (as in the 'spleen' poems) as well as 'evil'; moreover, in his dedication of his book to Théophile Gautier, Baudelaire refers to his poems, punningly again, as 'ces fleurs maladives' ('these sickly flowers'). But clearly when using 'Les Fleurs du Mal' purely as a title, Baudelaire thought of 'Mal' in its abstract and general connotations (in about nine cases out of ten, Claude Pichois has noted, *OCP* I, p. 797, the word is given an initial capital letter), whereas 'mal' meaning 'illness' is, in common usage, nearly always particularised or qualified in some way – as, for instance, in 'le mal du siècle', or 'le mal dont nous souffrons'. Baudelaire's pun on 'fleurs' is rather more subtle than the obvious one on 'mal', but on reflection it seems clear that the two senses he has in mind can only be the following: his poems may be considered a *product* of evil, and in that sense to 'flower' from it; at the same time, like flowers, they are *adornments* of evil. Or, to put it more fully: his poems are 'flowers of evil' first of all by virtue of their depiction or illustration of the evil from which they derive; but secondly also, by showing that even a product of evil may be beautiful, *like* a flower, and that true poetry, by definition, beautifies whatever it may come into contact with. Both these senses are in fact combined in a phrase of Baudelaire's first, unfinished *Epilogue* for the *Fleurs du Mal* of 1861, in which he says, of the city he is contemplating from a hilltop, that in it 'every enormity flourishes as might a flower'. He does not here directly attribute the perception of the flower to the poet; but in the concluding lines of his second, equally unfinished version of the *Epilogue*, he offers, altogether more happily, this alternative metaphor for the idea implicit in the actual title 'Les Fleurs du Mal'; addressing his beloved city of Paris, and calling on its presiding 'Angels' as witnesses, he declares himself to have fulfilled his duty as 'a perfect alchemist and blessed soul': 'from the mere dross you have given me, I have fashioned gold', 'Tu m'as donné ta boue et j'en ai fait de l'or'. In a cognate but more perfunctory analogy, this time within the published poem *Le Soleil* (lines 17–18), Baudelaire declares of the poet that, like the sun of the title, he ennobles the destiny of even the vilest things. More obviously related, finally, to the title *Les Fleurs du Mal*, is this (disingenuous) apologia offered in another uncompleted fragment intended for the 1861 edition, in this case for its abortive prose preface:

The richest sectors of the poetic domain had for long been divided up among a number of illustrious poets. I thought it might prove diverting, and all the more agreeable in that the task was so difficult, to extract *beauty* from Evil. This whole book, essentially useless and totally innocent into the bargain, has been written with no other purpose than my own amusement, that of gratifying my passion for obstacles of all kinds.   (*OCP* I, p. 181)

This paragraph is for the most part patently insincere, in that it implies a wholly impersonal, uninvolved motivation for the writing of poems that we know on the contrary, from the desparately frank letter to Ancelle of February 1866 (see p. 6, above), to have been deeply self-expressive in intention. But in one important respect, Baudelaire does here display an acute awareness of his own originality: the phrase 'extraire la *beauté* du Mal' exactly describes his poetic practice in certain characteristic poems (*Une martyre*, *Une charogne*; see pp. 68 and 74, below) – his ability to *transmute*, through the power of poetic language and especially of metaphor, the ugly and even the vicious into the strangely beautiful.

Baudelaire's title for his book of poems has one interesting further aspect: it makes clear that he is far more closely related to the Realists he so derided than he would ever have cared to admit. For if beauty can derive from evil, it can surely derive from anything; anything, therefore, can become a proper subject for poetry, which is precisely the broad claim made, for literature in general, by the Realists and Naturalists. The one essential condition for such a theory, had already been anticipated by Baudelaire a full eight years before his choice (or endorsement) of the title 'Les Fleurs du Mal': the subject of the work of art (so runs the caveat), whatever that subject may be, must be handled with such reverence and skill that in the process it becomes *great* art. Here, then, in those same terms but as early as 1846, is Baudelaire, in his *Salon* of that year (*OCP* II, pp. 443–4), explaining his impossible dream of a fully comprehensive 'Museum of Love' (a concept which, incidentally, anticipates by a full century or so André Malraux' famous *Musée imaginaire*), in which everything remotely relevant to Love would have its place – from the fumbling tenderness of a St Teresa to the resolute debauchery of what Baudelaire calls the 'bored centuries'; thus his ideal museum would include not only Watteau's *Departure for the Island of Cythera*, but also the wretched colour prints that prostitutes hang up in their bedrooms – for with such an important subject, nothing is too trivial to be neglected; besides which – and this is Baudelaire's conclusion, recalling, if more felicitously, the couplet above-summarised from *Le Soleil* – 'le génie sanctifie toutes choses', 'genius makes all things holy'; even from evil, beauty may freely flower. Thus, with Baudelaire and *Les Fleurs du Mal*, Realism, in this sense at least, enters poetry, too, at the level of great art.

Chapter 3

Sound and sense

The sound of French poetry

Sound is super-important in poetry – which obviously, by the mere fact of its typographical lay-out, is meant for the ear as well as the eye; indeed, we know the earliest poets to have *spoken* rather than written down their poems, to an audience gathered in public, and later poets are simply going back to this tradition each time they measure out their verses in rhythm and rhyme – for an audience which has now become private, but which still needs to register attentively that measured sound, equally with the sense it simultaneously conveys. No English-speaking reader, certainly, attempting to master the intricacies of French versification, can properly do so without first *hearing* the poems with which he or she is concerned. (To take the relevant analogy of music: who, after all, in order to register and appreciate the *sound* of a symphony, would be content to read a musical treatise or a programme note only, in preference to hearing the work actually performed?) The first requirement, therefore, in such a case, is that one should *listen* to as much French poetry as possible, in reliable performances by qualified speakers and teachers – armed only, initially at least, with that absolute minimum of basic information which will allow one to make sense of the new, unfamiliar conventions. And next, one should try oneself to speak French poems aloud, preferably with some expert guidance; the poems need not necessarily be those already previously heard, but could include others also, in the rendering of which one may begin to apply the practical skills one will by now have started to learn.

My first two minimum basic principles of traditional French versification (as laid down in the sixteenth and seventeenth centuries), relate to metre and stress. As far as metre is concerned, the important thing to remember is that the unit of measurement is here the individual *syllable* alone. This does not mean that in French poetry all syllables carry equal emphasis − on the contrary; but the variety of effect is certainly diminished, as compared with English poetry, by the fact that in ordinary French speech the stress (normally reinforced by an upward intonation) falls regularly on the last full, sounded syllable of a word or group of words: 'Vous comprenez / ce que je veux dire, / n'est-ce pas?' (To put it differently, one 'leans' here on the final syllable both by sounding it more strongly than the preceding ones, and by raising the pitch of one's voice.) As in English poetry, however, what determines the actual rhythm of the individual line (rhythm as opposed to metre) is the number and incidence of main stresses or tonic accents. Thus in the classical twelve-syllable alexandrine (by far the commonest metre in French verse) we have four tonic accents, four main stresses, corresponding to normal speech accents; the second and fourth of these stresses fall prescriptively on the sixth and twelfth syllables, with more freedom being allowed to the intermediate (first and third) stresses − as may be seen from these two Baudelaire examples, the first being slightly more conventional than the second:

La diane chantait / dans les cours des casern(es) . . .   1
(*Le Crépuscule du matin*)
Un cygne qui s'était / évadé de sa cag(e) . . .   17
(*Le Cygne*)

My third cardinal principle relates again to the alexandrine (as also to that other longer standard metre in French verse, the decasyllable), and concerns the normative main division in the line, called the caesura; this, requiring a very slight pause, occurs at the midway point of the line − i.e., in the alexandrine, after the sixth syllable and the second main stress:

Je respire l'odeur / de ton sein chaleureux . . .   2
(*Parfum exotique*)

The fourth of these principles is particularly important to remember, for the native French speaker no less than for the non-French reader, since it is peculiar to poetry and disappeared otherwise from ordinary Parisian usage some four centuries ago, at the end of the sixteenth century. This is the articulation of the mute or atonic e, when not elided before another vowel or unless occurring at the end of a line. In the next example, from *La Muse malade*, the normally mute e in 'froides' is sounded, whereas those at the end of 'folie' (preceding another vowel) and 'taciturnes' (coming at the end of the line) remain, as in ordinary speech, *un*sounded:

> La foli(e) et l'horreur, / froides et taciturn(es).   4

(I have similarly underlined the sounded atonic e's, and parenthesised the unsounded ones, in the previous examples quoted.)

Last of all, in this summary of the minimum basic principles of French versification, I should mention a further poetic practice absent from everyday speech, though not from the formal reading of prose; this is the elision of the final consonant of a word when this precedes (except at the caesura) an initial vowel in the word immediately ensuing:

> Se tenait à la barre / et coupait le flot noir . . .   18
> (*Don Juan aux enfers*)

Needless to say, there exist also numerous other rules which French poets traditionally observe (or have on occasion dared to infringe); but these can, I feel, be disregarded to begin with by the English-speaking reader anxious to immerse himself or herself as soon as possible in the rewarding sound-world of French poetry. One further practical warning may, however, be found useful: this concerns the frequent adaptation, by French poets, of normal pronunciation to metrical requirements − an adaptation the reader will be expected to allow for or to take into account when attending to the rhythm of a particular line. One common such example is the breaking-up of a diphthong into its component vowels:

Tes yeux creux sont peuplés de vi/si/ons nocturn(es) . . .   2
(*La Muse malade*)

The twelve-syllable alexandrine metre here requires 'visions' to be pronounced as if it had three syllables, rather than the two ('vi/sions') of ordinary speech; but the reader who has accustomed himself or herself to the alexandrine rhythm (or who, in the process of initiation, has been careful to count the syllables in the line!) will readily make the necessary accommodation, in this case as in others.

A final item of guidance applies generally to all readers of poetry, in whatever language, attempting analysis of its sound-effects. Such sound-effects are linked invariably to the *meanings* built into words by centuries of literary and spoken usage, and it is thus highly misleading to attribute the specific ideas, images or emotions that may be evoked by a passage of poetry, to particular sounds (sibilant or fricative consonants, combined or lengthened vowels, and so on), taken in isolation and supposedly expressive purely in themselves. Here as so often the definitive word has been spoken by Samuel Johnson, who over two centuries ago gave this admirably concise refutation of what I have elsewhere called (in *Sound and Sense in French Poetry*, pp. 5–6) 'the fallacy of expressive sound': 'It is scarcely to be doubted, that on many occasions we make the music which we imagine ourselves to hear; that we modulate the poem by our own disposition, and ascribe to the numbers the effects of the sense'.

The sound of Baudelaire's poetry

As it happens, few poets have been as attentive as Baudelaire to the sound of their own poetry. As a young man he liked greatly to recite his poems to his friends, who indeed mostly knew these poems only in this oral form; what is more, he seems to have felt a positive need, as part of the creative process, to speak his poems aloud at some preliminary stage, as if by this means alone could he fully test their effectiveness. In this habitual recitation of his verses he was much aided, by all accounts, by having a particularly beautiful, versatile and rhythmically cadenced voice — at times grave, intense and deep, at others more lightly pitched with an almost chanting delivery, at others, again, having a precise, cutting, even metallic quality, to match the poem's content. But Baudelaire is equally rare among great poets in recognising the importance, for the reader also, of the speaking-aloud of his verses. There is in this respect a fascinating parenthesis, interpolated in a letter of 18 March 1857 to his publisher, Poulet-Malassis, regarding the proper punctuation of his poems: 'As to my punctuation, remember that it is designed to indicate not only the sense of the words, but also the manner of their DECLAMATION' (*CPl* I, p. 384). It would be fascinating to single out from *Les Fleurs du Mal* a whole number of particular examples of this 'declamatory' style of punctuation on Baudelaire's part — but one such example must suffice to illustrate his point, that of the reiterated commas in the eighth line of *Le Beau Navire*, occurring at the precise moment, as it happens, when he explains the poem's title-metaphor — likening the woman's languid, wide-skirted grace of carriage to that of a proud ship casting gently, slowly, lazily off to sea under full sail: 'Suivant un rythme doux, et paresseux, et lent'.

To characterise for the English-speaking reader the particular sound of Baudelaire's poetry, a profitable first approach may be to consider his choice of individual metres; such an approach is crucial in that it is metre that determines rhythm, which in turn is no doubt the most important element of all in poetic sound. Baudelaire's most favoured metre by far is that of the classical twelve-syllabled alexandrine: its sonorous amplitude and measured, unhurried development, its symmetrical balance imparted by the (normally) central division at the caesura, are suited admirably to the complex richness of his imagery and thought. As a first example of his use of this metre, I take this paradisal seascape from *La Vie antérieure*, in which the self-reflected colours of the sunset blend mellifluously into the waves' deep resonant swell and rich solemn 'chords':

> Les houles, en roulant les images des cieux,
> Mêlaient d'une facon solennelle et mystique
> Les tout-puissants accords de leur riche musique
> Aux couleurs du couchant reflété par mes yeux.   8

The alexandrine, as handled by Baudelaire, seems especially suited to the evocation of wide, open vistas on land and sea; in the second quatrain from *Avec ses vêtements ondoyants et nacrés* . . . , the rolling waves recur, but in combination this time with the endless monotony of the desert, both seen as analogies for the cold, inhuman indifference of the admired mistress:

> Comme le sable morne et l'azur des déserts,
> Insensibles tous deux à l'humaine souffrance,
> Comme les longs réseaux de la houle des mers,
> Elle se développe avec indifférence.   8

In a different register, but still within the ambience of the eye held, entranced, by the loved one's successive 'poses', come these lines from *Les Bijoux*, in which the undulations of the alexandrine rhythm pass visibly into the very text:

> Et son bras et sa jambe, et sa cuisse et ses reins,
> Polis comme de l'huile, onduleux comme un cygne,
> Passaient devant mes yeux clairvoyants et sereins . . .   19

(Her arms and her legs, her back and her thighs, glistening like oil, sinuous like a swan, passed before my eyes, clear-sighted and serene . . .)

A final alexandrine example, from *Chant d'automne*, demonstrates Baudelaire's adroit manipulation of the caesura, by here placing it (through syntax and punctuation) after the second rather than the sixth syllable – the better thereby to emphasise the uncertainty in his mind as, in the third line here quoted (line 15), a disturbing question briefly poses itself to him ('That lulling, monotonous sound outside could be the nailing-up of a coffin; for whom?'), only to be as quickly evaded as 'mysterious', or transposed into another context (that of the dying season: summer declining into autumn), in the remainder of the stanza:

Il me semble, bercé par ce choc monotone,
Qu'on cloue en grande hâte un cercueil quelque part.
Pour qui? – C'était hier l'été; voici l'automne!
Ce bruit mystérieux sonne comme un départ.   16

In the slightly briefer decasyllable metre, the rhythm has a
more perceptible lilt and swaying balance – nowhere more
magically than in these images of the flowered and scented
Paradise into which, within their couches deep as tombs and
against a pastel background of pink and blue, the lovers of
La Mort des amants die together in a single long flash or sob
of ecstasy:

Nous aurons des lits pleins d'odeurs légères,
Des divans profonds comme des tombeaux,
Et d'étranges fleurs sur des étagères,
Ecloses pour nous sous des cieux plus beaux.   4

. . .

Un soir fait de rose et de bleu mystique,
Nous échangerons un éclair unique,
Comme un long sanglot, tout chargé d'adieux . . .   11

But it is the octosyllable rather than the decasyllable which,
among Baudelaire's metres, is next in frequency to the alexandrine. Here he is not always as successful as in the longer
forms: the too-swiftly recurrent rhythms, the need at times
for an almost staccato accentuation, impose perhaps an undue restraint on his freedom of expression. A notable failure
in this respect is the piece *Abel et Caïn*, with its awkwardly
stressed and altogether too mechanical sequence of alternately
rhyming couplets; against this example, however, may be set
such entire successes as *Tout entière*, *Le Vampire* and *Le Jet
d'eau* – to which one might add, especially, *Les Hiboux*,
which, with its elegant concision, achieves the rare feat of
rendering didacticism acceptable to modern tastes.
   Baudelaire's metrical schemes are by no means always
uniform and constant from beginning to end; where the subject seems to invite this, he is fond of contriving asymmetrical
combinations which arrest expectation and surprise the ear,

for instance by foreshortening certain cadences within a stanza.
A particularly happy example in this respect is furnished,
once again, by that prototypical 'amorous tribute', *Le Beau
Navire*, in which the short eight-syllabled third line interrupts
and accentuates, by its rapid 'bounce', the measured alexandrine tread of the other three lines of each quatrain. The
general strophic pattern adopted by Baudelaire in *Le Beau
Navire*, provides further interest: each of the first three stanzas is made to recur at different and strategic moments within
the poem — with the repetition of the first stanza as the
fourth, for instance, recalling to the reader's mind the idea,
implanted at the very outset, of a 'diversity' of charms.

Repetition, in one form or another, is a key principle of
Baudelaire's art. The most obvious metrical device of this
kind, and the one most obviously related to song, is the
refrain; of the three poems by Baudelaire using this device:
Les Litanies de Satan, *Le Jet d'eau* and *L'Invitation au
voyage*, the last two are surpassing masterpieces. The more
conventional of the two, at least in its 'gallant' theme, is *Le
Jet d'eau*. Here, between each eight-line octosyllable stanza
developing its symmetrical series of long sentences evoking
the amorous idyll, the poet interposes, in a beautifully poised
six-line refrain in which the lines are alternately of six and
four syllables only, his picture of the iridescent fountain, rising and falling in the courtyard outside. The sound-pattern in
L'Invitation au voyage is more unusual, and demands detailed analysis as a privileged illustration of Baudelaire's metrical
art. A first anomaly is that in both the main stanzas and the
refrain each line carries an odd rather than an even number
of syllables — the three main stanzas of twelve lines each,
grouped three by three in a 5:5:7 design (i.e. two five-syllabled
lines followed by one of seven), being rounded off by a two-
line refrain also of seven syllables but having a quite different
rhythm. This difference of rhythm springs from the fact that
these two lines, unlike those in the main stanzas, have three
rather than two tonic accents — as may be seen from this
sequence in which the last six lines of the first stanza are
followed by the first refrain:

Les soleils mouillés
De ces ciels brouillés
Pour mon esprit ont les charmes
Si mystérieux
De tes traîtres yeux,
Brillant à travers leurs larmes.

12

Là, tout n'est qu'ordre et beauté,
Luxe, calme et volupté.

(In that country whose humid suns and blurred skies have the same mysterious charms as your insidious eyes shining through their tears, everything is order and beauty, luxury, calm and delight.)

An additional factor here is the virtual absence in the refrain of sounded mute e's; with one exception, the second syllable of 'luxe', all the vowel sounds have full sonority. This sustained fullness of vowel sounds gives great amplitude and resonance to the refrain − very appropriately, in what is in effect a sort of rapt incantation, a litany of magic virtues. Full vowels are in fact predominant throughout the whole poem, but they are felt rather less strongly in the main verses, where the restriction to two tonic accents only, creates in certain lines (3, 9, 12, 17, 20, 31, 34, 37), in which a considerable number of syllables have to be accommodated within a small compass, an effect of rapidity and lightness. In one indeed of these lines (34), through the unexpected interpolation of a mute e within a sequence of full vowels, we even get an effect similar to that of syncopation in music; the reference here is to the ships returning from the farthest ends of the earth to gratify the beloved's every whim: 'Qu'ils viennent / du bout du monde.'

Another device of metrical repetition, employed by Baudelaire in four poems of the greatest beauty: *Le Balcon*, *Réversibilité*, *Mœsta et errabunda* and *Lesbos*, is often described as the *repetend*. Here, the first line of each stanza recurs more or less identically as the fifth and last, imparting to the poem as a whole a sort of cyclical regularity within irregularity. In each of these four cases, the *repetend* seems to hold a special appropriateness to its subject. In *Le Balcon*, the reiterated lines appear by the end of the poem to have been sounding an almost obsessive note, tempering grateful recollection of the past with uneasy speculation about the future: is it *still* within our power, Baudelaire asks his 'mother of memories' and 'mistress of mistresses', to revive and re-create past happiness, as well as to recall it fondly? In *Réversibilité*, the anxiety becomes explicit: the repetitions are the equivalent of a feverish hand outstretched again and again to seek, as if by the theological analogy of the 'reversible' transmission of virtues, understanding, compassion, reassurance from a loved one whose whole radiant person seems so dishearteningly distant from the poet's own, locked as it is in anguish, hatred and infirmity. In *Mœsta et errabunda*, the note of anxiety has receded, though the hope of consolation (in this case through imagined departures in space and time) remains no less forlorn; the repeated questions and exclamations have an initial urgency as they invite the woman's mind to cast itself across the distant oceans, then of elegiac regret as the poet's thoughts turn to a now irretrievable past. In *Lesbos*, last of the four, the *repetend* continually buoys up and sustains the fervent, exalted hymn, as it defiantly asserts the sacred island's claims to a rival and *valid* sexuality. It is notable, as I have said, that all four of these poems utilise the five-line stanza, which Baudelaire seems particularly to have favoured for long-breathed and impassioned apostrophes; this form recurs in *La Chevelure*, though here without the *repetend* structure framing and enclosing each stanza; once again, though, the elastic bounds of the poet's imagination re-create, in close, remembered detail, an idyllic and exotic past. But the supreme example of Baudelaire's metrical virtuosity is surely *Harmonie du soir*. Here he adopts and modifies a Malayan verse-form, the *pantoum*, in which the second and fourth lines of each quatrain become, in an intricate web of sound, the first and third lines of the next. As an added refinement from the aural point of view, Baudelaire here succeeds in capturing the very lilt of the 'melancholy waltz' named in his fourth and again his seventh line:

Voici / venir les temps / où vibrant / sur sa tige
Chaque fleur / s'évapo / re ainsi / qu'un encensoir;
Les sons / et les parfums / tour / nent dans l'air du soir;
Val / se mélancoli / que et langoureux / vertige!

(Evening has come: it is the moment when each flower vibrates on its stem and sheds its perfume like a censer − when the sounds and scents swirl together in a languorous and melancholy waltz.)

In general, Baudelaire in his verse-forms favoured the shorter poem (later rationalising this choice by invoking, *OCP* II, p. 332, the theories of Poe), rather than the longer structures, often of epic proportions, preferred by his Romantic predecessors. A particular predilection was for the sonnet − a genre which in the 1830s and 1840s, thanks mainly to the practical advocacy of Sainte-Beuve and Gautier, was beginning to experience something of a revival from its Renaissance heyday. It is here significant that in his semi-autobiographical novella of 1843–6, *La Fanfarlo*, Baudelaire should have identified his 'other self', Samuel Cramer, specifically as the author of a collection of sonnets, *Les Orfraies*, which, as described in the novella, bear a strong resemblance to certain poems of *Les Fleurs du Mal*. Almost half of the poems in that book are, in point of fact, in sonnet form: many of them are among Baudelaire's finest compositions, exhibiting not only the characteristic qualities of the genre − its challenging concision, its economy of rhyme, its clear division into two parts (octave, sestet; two quatrains, then two tercets), the opportunities it affords for clinching wit at the close − but also, idiosyncratically, a more fluid, less sharply chiselled character than is usual. Baudelaire retained his admiration for the sonnet throughout his life: not only did he choose eleven poems specifically of this type to send in to *Le Messager de l'assemblée* in April 1851, as 'trailers' for his forthcoming *Limbes* collection, but also, some nine years later, in a letter to Armand Fraisse concerning the poems of an admired contemporary, Joséphin Soulary, he delivers this perceptive tribute to what he calls the 'Pythagorean beauty' of the sonnet: precisely because its form is so restrictively laconic (he asserts), it confers added intensity on the ideas it embodies; its beauty is that of some intricately worked metal or mineral, and yet it is comprehensively versatile (*CPl* I, p. 676). In this respect, it is particularly interesting that Baudelaire should have elected to return to the form in four masterly sonnets of the late 1850s and early 1860s:

Semper eadem, *A une passante*, *La Fin de la journée* ('At the Day's End') and *Recueillement*. Even in his earlier, relatively unadventurous efforts in this genre, Baudelaire had rarely chosen to follow with rigid exactness the conventional rhyme-schemes of Renaissance models; now, in the four later sonnets, we note a more substantial development in another and this time structural dimension: the sweeping aside altogether of the traditional separation of octave and sestet, in favour either of a division postponed until after the beginning of the sestet (as in *A une passante* and *Recueillement*), or of a single uninterrupted argument maintained over the whole fourteen lines (as in *Semper eadem* and *La Fin de la journée*). Significantly, since in another letter of February 1860, ad-dressed this time directly to Soulary (*CPl* I, p. 679), Baudelaire praises that poet for his exploitation of the 'dramatic' qualities of the sonnet, each of the four later poems above-named captures remarkably the speaking *vividness* of the personal situations they transcribe. This is nowhere more striking, perhaps, than in the bold innovations of *Recueillement*, in which Baudelaire does not merely 'overlap' from his second quatrain to his first tercet, but 'runs on', metrically and syntactically, from the one to the other; the pause between the two stanzas is thus dramatically reduced, and the quiet final episode in which the poet, with his imagined 'companion', turns away from the hectic, pleasure-greedy city depicted in lines 5–7, is strategically delayed until after the (irregularly early) caesura in the ninth line.

This last example, from *Recueillement*, of stanza-straddling enjambment, leads on naturally to a consideration of Baudelaire's whole treatment of this feature of traditional metrics. As in the case of sonnet-structure, there are here clear chronological implications. In the earliest of his poems Baudelaire was careful to observe traditional rules of ver-sification, including the end-stopping of lines to avoid any run-on from the one to the next; a case in point is *Le Crépuscule du matin*, one of the earliest-composed of all the poems in *Les Fleurs du Mal*. Increasingly after 1843, however, Baudelaire seems to have been ready to infringe this prohibition; a considerably more adventurous example of enjambments from one line to another, is to be found in the companion poem (no doubt rather later composed), *Le Crépuscule du soir*, whilst in *Le Vampire* and *L'Amour et le crâne* (both published only in 1855) Baudelaire goes a stage further still, daring to run on from one *stanza* to another. But for his most audacious experiments in stanzaic enjambment we must await three poems composed after 1858, and all ultimately dedicated, as it happens, to Victor Hugo: *Le Cygne*, *Les Sept Vieillards*, *Les Petites Vieilles*. In the last of these, Baudelaire ends his fourth stanza, evoking the pathetic movements of the 'little old ladies' of his title (trotting, dragging themselves to and fro, jigging unwittingly up and down with little dancing steps), with the first phrase of a quite new sentence – a phrase which remains unintelligible until it has found its completion at the beginning of the next quatrain:

. . . Tout cassés   16

Qu'ils sont, ils ont des yeux perçants comme une vrille,
Luisants comme ces trous où l'eau dort dans la nuit . . .

(Utterly disjointed though their limbs may be, their eyes still retain the piercing sharpness of gimlets, and shine out like puddles glistening in the dark . . .)

Le Crépuscule du matin (mentioned near the beginning of the previous paragraph) is in rhyming alexandrine couplets; this verse-form – the 'most hallowed' in French verse, as Graham Chesters has rightly remarked (*Baudelaire and the Poetics of Craft*, p. 152) – is to be found in a number of other poems of Baudelaire's early period, though he was soon to abandon it in favour of forms based on quatrains, with alternating or 'enclosing' rhymes of the *abab* or *abba* type, or on other strophic combinations. Another striking development in the domain of rhyme, was Baudelaire's abandonment, in his later verses, of the 'rich rhymes' on which he earlier prided himself. (By 'richness' in this context is meant the linkage in rhyme of three or more concordant elements – two consonants enclosing a vowel, for instance.) The most spectacular example of such rhyming in *Les Fleurs du Mal* is to be found in *Sed non satiata* ('Still Unsatisfied'), in which, in the quatrains (as Albert Cassagne has pointed out, *Versification et métrique de Charles Baudelaire*, pp. 13–14), Baudelaire contrived to use up all the rhymes in ' –avane' existing in the French language. Altogether more impressive poetically, however, are the rich rhymes of *A une mendiante rousse* ('To a Red-haired Beggar-girl'; a charming fantasy, even though disparaged in 1851 by Baudelaire himself), and above all, of the haunting *Parfum exotique*:

> Guidé par ton odeur vers de charmants climats,
> Je vois un port rempli de voiles et de mâts
> Encor tout fatigués par la vague marine,   11
>
> Pendant que le parfum des verts tamariniers,
> Qui circule dans l'air et m'enfle la narine,
> Se mêle dans mon âme au chant des mariniers.   14

(Guided by your perfume, I see also a seaport crowded with sails and masts still battered from the waves, and fill my nostrils with the scent of the tamarind trees, and hear, mingling with it all, the song of the sailors singing away in their ships.)

In all three of these developments, then: his loosening of the sonnet structure, his extension of the techniques of enjambment, his readiness to rhyme less 'richly' and elaborately, Baudelaire displays a clear trend of decided general importance. It is significant, in this respect, that each of these innovatory procedures of his should have coincided with his experiments, from 1857 onwards, in the writing of a whole series of prose poems. In an article of November 1851, Baudelaire ranges himself by ironic implication among 'all those rascals who run up debts and actually believe that a poet's task is to express lyrical feeling in rhythms laid down by tradition' (*OCP* II, p. 39); eight years later, he is still pursuing this same lyrical ambition, but his medium has become either the wholly untraditional prose poem or the 'liberated' verse of such texts of 1859 as *Le Voyage*, *Le Cygne*, *Les Sept Vieillards*, *Les Petites Vieilles*. Concerning the last but one of these Baudelaire was indeed to wonder, in a letter to his friend

Jean Morel (*CPl* I, p. 583), whether in writing them he had not simply overstepped 'the limits assigned to poetry'. All in all, it is as if, at this final stage of his career, Baudelaire had felt he could no longer contain his poetic ideas within conventional bounds, but needed to shake off some at least of the restrictions he now felt to be cramping the expression of those 'mouvements lyriques de l'âme'; we seem already, in these later verses, to be looking forward to the time, only twenty-five years or so distant, when certain French poets (Laforgue, Kahn, with Rimbaud as precursor) will break free entirely from the shackles of conventional prosody, and embark resolutely on the most radical metrical experiment of all, free verse.

So much for the traditionally measurable elements of Baudelaire's poetic sound-world: its metre, rhythm and rhyme. Equally important are two less easily quantifiable features: tone and tempo, which are none the less instantly recognisable and characteristic. By tone I mean literally tone of *voice* – the way we modulate words in uttering them, to convey a particular emotional colouring. Tone is determined to some extent by choice of vocabulary, but above all by context; compare such a phrase as 'You're an idiot!', spoken in a hostile way to someone with whom one is angry, and 'You're an idiot', spoken in a caressing and indulgent way to someone one loves. In poetry, the context is simply the whole poem, and an excellent illustration of Baudelaire's command of tone (and of the way, incidentally, in which one should speak his verse) is provided by the sonnet *Semper eadem*. As in the three other love poems I earlier linked with this one, under the heading 'The Death of the Heart', Baudelaire is here striving to explain to the perennially radiant woman of the title ('Ever the Same') that for him, as for so many others, the bitter harvest of love has left only an unmysterious sadness, a longing to retreat from all threatening passion into the half-death of tranquillity and repose. In this intimate context his twice-repeated injunction to her: 'Taisez-vous!' (overlapping from the second quatrain to the first tercet, be it noted in the light of my previous comments on Baudelaire's

sonnet-technique in his later years), is not in any way to be interpreted as an angry admonition ('Shut *up*!'), but rather, as
the preceding words clearly indicate, as a gentle, indulgent,
half-teasing rebuke, in response to the probings of a cap-
tivating voice to which, alas! he can no longer fully respond.
This tone of appealing, persuasive argumentation is sustained
throughout other poems, too: in a more urgently despairing
key, in *Réversibilité* and, on the other hand, in the third sonnet, *Le Cadre* , of the decasyllable sequence *Un fantôme*, in a
serene retrospect addressed to the reader rather than to the
woman herself. A deeper, more conventionally amorous feeling pervades *L'Invitation au voyage*; here, the tone throughout
is vibrant, caressing, insistent, *warm* – like the warm light that
floods over the landscape at the end of the final stanza.

A quite different tone, one of aggression and frustrated
grievance, may be heard in several others of Baudelaire's love
poems (or perhaps one should here say, of his love–hate
poems) – as for instance in the two lines, with their vehement
sweep of 'attack', as Marcel Ruff has called it (*Baudelaire*, p.
135), which open *Le Vampire* and lead on, two stanzas later,
to a culminating curse:

> Toi qui, comme un coup de couteau,
> Dans mon cœur plaintif es entrée . . .
>
> . . .
>
> – Maudite, maudite sois-tu!   12

(You who like a knife have plunged your way into my plaintive
heart . . . twice accurséd be you!)

Eloquence is a staple tone adopted by Baudelaire in many
of his later poems; he does not scorn, on occasion, high
classical rhetoric, as in the vibrant concluding stanzas of *Les
Petites Vieilles*, in which can almost be heard the elaborate
ringing cadences of a sermon by Bossuet:

> Ruines! ma famille! ô cerveaux congénères!
> Je vous fais chaque soir un solennel adieu!
> Où serez-vous demain, Eves octogénaires,
> Sur qui pèse la griffe effroyable de Dieu?   84

(O kindred, ailing creatures! Each night I bid you a solemn farewell! For where tomorrow will you be, eighty-year-old daughters of Eve, over whom God poises already his terrifying claw?)

In *Le Masque* the rhetoric is altogether less successful — caricatural almost, if one imagines the stylised gestures which would accompany its insistent button-holing, Ancient-Mariner-like, of the reader invited to contemplate the statue with its two faces, false and true. More happily, in other texts, rhetoric is employed to further a moral or metaphysical argument — in *Lesbos* and in the first *Femmes damnées* poem (*Delphine et Hippolyte*), in the sonnet *Le Gouffre*, in *Le Goût du néant*. A word should here be added concerning certain typical instances of a 'feline' ambiguity of tone (the epithet was first applied to Baudelaire's poetry by Swinburne; see Patricia Clements, *Baudelaire and the English Tradition*, p. 34); in these cases an unchanged smoothness of delivery subtly conceals or 'muffles' the sudden introduction of an alien, discordant note. A prime instance of this may be found in the opening lines of *Le Crépuscule du soir*:

> Voici le soir charmant, ami du criminel;
> Il vient comme un complice, à pas de loup; le ciel
> Se ferme lentement comme une grande alcôve,
> Et l'homme impatient se change en bête fauve.   4

(Evening has come, the charming evening, the criminal's delight: it has come on stealthy feet, like an accomplice; slowly, the sky closes like some great alcove, and impatient Man turns into a wild beast.)

As one's voice, after the deceptively bland 'charmant' and 'ami', comes to the end of the first line, the word 'criminel' is suddenly introduced, with all its sinister associations underlined by the sharp initial consonant and snarling final syllable; the whole spirit and atmosphere have now changed, and the night, within the urban jungle, has become full of menace. A similar technique is adopted (as Marcel Ruff, again, has noted, *Baudelaire*, pp. 139–40) in a further set of opening lines, those of the famous *Une charogne*:

>   Rappelez-vous l'objet que nous vîmes, mon âme,
>   Ce beau matin d'été si doux:
>   Au détour d'un sentier une charogne infâme
>   Sur un lit semé de cailloux . . .   4

(Do you recall, my beloved, that *thing* we once saw together, on a beautiful summer morning? At a turning of the path, on a bed of pebbles, that hideous *carcase* lying there before us?)

The word 'objet', almost at the poem's beginning, brings a momentary unease — but this is dispelled initially by the reminder of the surpassing beauty of that summer day; it is not until the third line that the true horror reveals itself, with the brutal phrase 'une charogne infâme', startling the reader just as the sudden sight of the carcase must have startled Baudelaire and his mistress on that gentle country walk. But a still more dramatic, still more adroitly sinister example of such manipulations of tone, is to be found in *Une martyre*. Who, reading the luxuriant first two stanzas of this poem, would be prepared for the revelations of the five that follow, with their meticulous depiction — as if of some martyred saint transposed to a contemporary setting (the subtitle reads, ironically, 'Sketch by an Unknown Master'), and all the more shocking for being so lovingly prolonged — of the exquisite female corpse, in its nudity, lying within that elegant boudoir, its severed head reposing, flower-like, on the bedtable alongside, disgorging on the greedy pillow its stream of red, living blood?

   The other non-measurable, contextually defined feature of Baudelaire's poetic sound-world, tempo, may be more briefly considered. To some extent, of course, tempo is determined by metre: we have seen already, in analysing *L'Invitation au voyage* pp. 58–9, above), that the *impair* line, by its irregular accentual patterns, often creates rapidity, and this is true also, though less strikingly, of many of Baudelaire's octosyllabic poems; the alexandrine, on the other hand, tends by its very nature to unfold with grave and measured deliberation. Even in a twelve-syllable line, however, the heightened drama of a situation may quicken the tempo, at least momentarily. A particularly notable example of this is to be

found in *Don Juan aux enfers*, with its unhurried narration, in
the first two quatrains, of the 'calm hero''s journey of damnation towards the underworld, quite unheeding (as we learn at
the end of the poem) of the 'herd' of his past female victims lift-
ing their voices in execration from the shore. But suddenly, at
the ninth line, a quite different voice, that of the irrepressible
Sganarelle, briefly interrupts the solemn litany of accusations:

> Sganarelle en riant lui réclamait ses gages,
> Tandis que Don Luis avec un doigt tremblant
> Montrait à tous les morts errant sur les rivages
> Le fils audacieux qui railla son front blanc.   12

(The laughing Sganarelle was there, too, to demand his wages –
whilst the white-haired Don Luis, with a trembling finger, pointed
out to others of the dead wandering on the banks of the river Styx,
the audacious son who had dared to mock him.)

It would be quite absurd to read the first of these quoted lines
in the slower, graver tempo appropriate to the others; the very
characterisation of Sganarelle, to say nothing of the profu-
sion of words within the line, demand that it be spoken (or
heard in the mind) as a sort of rapid, irreverent patter. In my
second example, from *Les Bijoux*, what here quickens the
rhythm is not so much the dramatic context as the dazzling
visual stimulus suddenly impinging upon the poet's rapt con-
templation of the woman in her nakedness:

> Quand il jette en dansant son bruit vif et moqueur,
> Ce monde rayonnant de métal et de pierre
> Me ravit en extase, et j'aime à la fureur
> Les choses où le son se mêle à la lumière.   8

(This whole shining world of metal and precious stone, as it dances
before my eyes with its dazzling and mocking chime, ravishes me into ecstasy, for I love to distraction all things in which light mingles
with sound.)

The first and second lines quoted here, in their second accele-
rated tempo and mounting excitement, cast suddenly into
our eyes (as into his) the sound and spectacle of the jewels
adorning her person; but with the third line, the brilliant
image is assimilated back into the total picture, and the tempo

slows to the calm, sensuous enjoyment of treasured retrospection.

Imagery

One of the great glories of *Les Fleurs du Mal* is the extraordinary richness and originality (remarked on by a few perceptive contemporaries) of its figurative imagery. I do not consider it a very profitable approach to seek to classify these effects in terms of their grammatical presentation (is this a cautious simile, is that a more audacious metaphor?) – even though it may be true, as a chronological observation, that Baudelaire's earliest poems, such as *Le Crépuscule du matin*, did include more similes than metaphors. But for the most part it was probably the sheer requirements of metre that determined the mode of presentation in this respect; whether or not he introduced a particular image with a 'comme' or an 'ainsi' or a 'semblable à', will have depended above all simply on whether the line required a further syllable or two to fill it out, or whether a more telescoped, metaphoric image would better fit the metrical scheme. But in any case it is not the particular mechanism of transference from the literal to the figurative that most strikes the reader of *Les Fleurs du Mal*; it is the remarkable acuity and range of Baudelaire's sensory responses, as attested by the images themselves and, most strikingly of all, by the frequent, 'synaesthetic' intermingling of one sense with another:

> Les parfums, les couleurs et les sons se répondent.   8
>
> Il est des parfums frais comme des chairs d'enfants,
> Doux comme les hautbois, verts comme les prairies . . .

(Scents, colours and sounds give answer to one another. There are scents that are as delicate as the touch of children's flesh, as sweet as the sound of oboes, as green as the grass of meadows . . .)
                                                    (*Correspondances*)

> Les sons et les parfums tournent dans l'air du soir . . .   3

(Sounds and scents swirl together in the evening air . . .)
                                                    (*Harmonie du soir*)

«O métamorphose mystique
De tous mes sens fondus en un !
Son haleine fait la musique,
Comme sa voix fait le parfum!»   24

(O mystical metamorphosis of all my senses fused into one — her
breath transformed into music, her voice into perfume!)

(*Tout entière*)

The initial example quoted above reminds us that Baudelaire
was perhaps the first poet, in France or elsewhere, to explore
fully the potentialities of olfactory images — so tenacious in
their power to stay in the mind and to summon up with total
vividness some episode in the past. Baudelaire's, indeed, must
be the most receptive and unforgetful nose in all poetic
history! But his other senses, too, were equally alert and
responsive — that of hearing, for instance:

Quel démon a doté la mer, rauque chanteuse
Qu'accompagne l'immense orgue des vents grondeurs,
De cette fonction sublime de berceuse?   9

(What demon has bestowed upon the sea, that rough-voiced singer
blending her voice to the vast, rumbling organ-swell of the winds, so
sublime a power to cradle us into sleep?)   (*Mœsta et errabunda*)

A comprehensive survey of all Baudelaire's sensory images
has been brilliantly provided by Lloyd Austin, in his
L'Univers poétique de Baudelaire; let me now, viewing these
images rather from the point of view of their content than
their derivation, single out in *Les Fleurs du Mal* one particular type of metaphor that no predecessor seems to have
developed as fully or individually. Such metaphors could be
called 'subjective', in that they render emotion through sensa-
tion with physiological exactness. Beginning with the more
general rather than the purely personal, I would first cite the
marvellous image whereby, in *Le Crépuscule du matin*,
Baudelaire conveys that deep sense of the transitory and
evanescent that, to the wakeful at dawn, seems everywhere
pervasive:

> Comme un visage en pleurs que les brises essuient,
> L'air est plein du frisson des choses qui s'enfuient . . .   10

(Like a tear-stained face drying in the wind, the air is filled with the tremor of things fleeing away . . .)

At a different time of day and in a different season, there is that edgy hypersensitivity of overcast summer days:

> Tu rappelles ces jours blancs, tièdes et voilés,
> Qui font se fondre en pleurs les cœurs ensorcelés,
> Quand, agités d'un mal inconnu qui les tord,
> Les nerfs trop éveillés raillent l'esprit qui dort.   8

(You bring to mind those somnolent days of warm veiled whiteness, which induce sudden, mysterious tears and strange, nervy lethargies.)

(Ciel brouillé)

As the day advances, nightfall comes once again, bringing with it not only anxiety but unnamed fears:

> . . . les vagues terreurs de ces affreuses nuits
> Qui compriment le cœur comme un papier qu'on froisse . . .4

(. . . vague terrors which grip the heart like paper crumpled in the hand . . .)   *(Réversibilité)*

More frightening still, there is the fear of the 'great hole' of sleep itself:

> J'ai peur du sommeil comme on a peur d'un grand trou . . .   9
> *(Le Gouffre)*

I have mentioned already, in speaking of Baudelaire's 'Death of the Heart' poems, the two extraordinary and elaborate images in *Causerie*, whereby he conveys his retrospective recoil from the ravages of passion − successively characterised as the marauding tooth and claw of Woman, and as a vengeful mob bent on destruction, invading the 'palace' of the poet's heart; in the opening quatrain of the same poem (as too, in very similar terms, in lines 46–8 of *Un voyage à Cythère*), the bitterness of past memories comes flooding back, in a still more vivid image, as if in the very taste felt in one's mouth.

In these latter instances (as in the two earlier quoted, from *Le Crépuscule du matin* and *Ciel brouillé*), Baudelaire applies a technique of which he showed full awareness in an article of 1861 on the nineteenth-century poetess Marceline Desbordes-Valmore (*OCP* II, p. 148) – that of going 'outside himself', so to speak, to imagine scenes or landscapes in external Nature which are the symbolic counterpart of his own feelings, thereby reversing the still more strongly established Romantic and pre-Romantic procedure of the *paysage d'âme* (also found in Baudelaire, in such poems as *Alchimie de la douleur* and *Horreur sympathique*), whereby a pre-existing spectacle in nature is felt to harmonise with the writer's mood. Many examples of this converse type of *âme-paysage*, nearly always characterising a mood of 'spleen', are to be found in *Les Fleurs du Mal*: in whole poems such as *De profundis clamavi* and the second of the four entitled *Spleen*, *J'ai plus de souvenirs que si j'avais mille ans* . . . ('I am burdened with more memories than if I had lived a thousand years . . .'), or in such incidental metaphors as those of *Chant d'automne*, lines 5–8, *Le Voyage*, lines 111–12, *Chanson d'après-midi*, lines 39–40, *La Destruction*, lines 10–11. But perhaps the most astonishing of all Baudelaire's subjective metaphors is that symmetrical series in which, with almost hysterical self-awareness, he dramatises in *L'Héautontimorouménos* the Spirit of Irony he detects within himself:

> Je suis la plaie et le couteau!
> Je suis le soufflet et la joue!
> Je suis les membres et la roue,
> Et la victime et le bourreau!   24

(I am the wound and the knife, the slap and the cheek that is slapped, the limbs and the wheel that breaks them, the victim and the executioner!)

From his earliest poems, Baudelaire's imagery seems strikingly new-fashioned: already, in *Le Crépuscule du matin*, one may single out his use of two boldy sanguinary and 'anti-aesthetic' similes to characterise everyday realities. In the first of these similes (lines 5–6), the lamplight contending with the daylight is preceded by a comparison (anticipating a famous sequence in the Surrealist film *Un Chien andalou*) with a bloodshot eye as it quivers and throbs; in the second (lines 19–20) − less gratuitous than the first, since borrowing its justification from the context as a whole − the distant cock-crow rending the misty air is equated with a choking sob clotted with blood. Still more original is a passage from another early poem, *Une charogne*, in which, by a reverse process, the repellent is paradoxically transmuted into the mysteriously beautiful. In this poem, as we have seen, Baudelaire inflicts upon his mistress the macabre reminder of the putrefying carcase they had once encountered, lying in their path, on a summer walk. At a certain point in his description, however (line 25), the noisome corpse is all at once transformed by analogy into images utterly remote: those of strange music, running water, the blowing wind, the swirling chaff scattered by a winnower, the blurred, forgotten sketch awaiting completion, from memory, on a painter's easel − only for brutal reality to reimpose itself once again, in line 33, in the form of the bitch-dog eyeing the carcase for its chance to snatch back the morsel it had been obliged to relinquish.

Although markedly an innovator in these and other figurative techniques, Baudelaire retained to the end an unexpected affection for one highly traditional mode of expression: the allegorical personification. Allegory in the wider sense, determining the structure of a whole poem and conferring upon its imagery a sustained figurative meaning, is to be found in many of the poems composed by him in his poetic heyday, the early and middle 1840s; but already here one notices a perceptible gradation, from such conventional Romantic structures as those of *L'Albatros*, *Le Mauvais Moine*, *La Cloche fêlée*, *Le Flacon* − first the image, then in a final part the 'explanation' of its significance − to the more complex interweaving of literal and figurative in *Le Tonneau de la Haine* ('Hatred as a Cask'), *L'Amour et le crâne*, *Duellum*, and most strikingly of all, *L'Ennemi*. In Baudelaire's later poems, this type of continued allegory is abandoned altogether; what still persists, however, often in the most unlikely contexts, is allegory in its abridged form of individual abstract personifications, identified by an initial capital letter. (In mediaeval poetry, of course, such capitalisation would serve to indicate one protagonist among many within a larger allegorical narrative.) Thus to the numerous such personifications already widespread throughout the first edition of 1857 of *Les Fleurs du Mal*, may be added the generally more subtle figures appearing in many later texts. These personifications in his later poems may on occasion obtrude (like the 'she-wolf' of Suffering, in lines 46–7 of *Le Cygne*); in general, however, they take on a strange elegance and grace which allow them to acclimatise quite naturally to a modern world of urban realism. A case in point is that of *Recueillement*, with its wholly successful blend of such stylised figures as the poet's faithful companion, Suffering; Evening, and its scourge of Pleasure lashing the febrile dwellers in the city; the bygone Years, smiling Regret, the dying Sun, gentle Night drawing its shroud audibly on, all combining to bring the sonnet to its calm, elegiac conclusion.

Irony and ambiguity, inasmuch as they are both related kinds of word-play involving the unexpected linkage of ideas (saying one thing and meaning another, in the first case; saying two things in one and meaning both, in the second) might well seem to belong equally here, under the global heading 'metaphor' (the bringing together through imagery of two normally separate things). Intentional ambiguity at the verbal level, however, despite Baudelaire's 'punning title' for *Les Fleurs du Mal* (see pp. 47–8, above), is rarely to be found in the book as a whole; irony is more common, as may be seen in such poems as *La Muse malade* and *La Muse vénale*, *La Béatrice* and *L'Imprévu*. Equally characteristic in Baudelaire is paradoxical antithesis (the linkage of two apparently incompatible ideas): Pleasure, for instance, as a merciless tormentor, in the example just quoted from *Recueillement*, or its pursuit as a form of atrocity, in *Les Aveugles* (line 12); the 'charming evening' which is also 'the criminal's friend', in *Le Crépuscule du soir* (line 1); the lovers 'prospering' in poverty in *La Lune offensée* ('The Affronted Moon', line 5).

But unexpected conjunctions of this kind come naturally to one of such inherently contra-suggestible temperament as Baudelaire; indeed they take us back, after all, to the central paradox of the whole book, or at least of its title: flowers not of good, but of evil.

I must add a word concerning one especially characteristic aspect of Baudelaire's non-figurative imagery in *Les Fleurs du Mal*: his strategic placing of general epithets which for all their semi-abstract character, seem mysteriously to open up infinitely wide sensory perspectives – as, for instance, in these few quotations taken almost at random, in which I have italicised the epithets in question:

> Comme de *longs* échos qui de loin se confondent
> Dans une *ténébreuse* et *profonde* unité,
> *Vaste* comme la nuit et comme la clarté,
> Les parfums, les couleurs et les sons se répondent.   8

(Like long echoes merging together from afar in a unity which is at once obscure and deep, and vast and bright, scents, colours and sounds give answer to one another.)   (*Correspondances*)

> Le ciel est *triste* et *beau* comme un grand reposoir.   8

(The sky is sad and beautiful, like some great processional altar.)
(*Harmonie du soir*)

> . . . cherchant, l'œil hagard,
> Les cocotiers *absents* de la *superbe* Afrique
> Derrière la muraille *immense* du brouillard . . .   44

(. . . her haggard eye seeking, beyond that vast wall of fog, the absent palm-trees of her proud, native Africa . . .)   (*Le Cygne)*

Structure

One thing that often shapes the structure of Baudelaire's poems is the varying modes of address he chooses. In this respect apostrophe affords a favoured means of approach; such a tactic is conventional enough in love poetry, which by definition is directly addressed to the object of that love, but Baudelaire extends the use of apostrophe to almost every possible subject and situation. Thus he may apostrophise his reader, himself, his own Muse, his own Suffering; a hanged man on an island (with whom he identifies); a red-haired beggar-girl, or a beautiful woman seen for a moment in a Paris street; the skeletons in a book of anatomical plates; the islands of Lesbos and Cythera; Nature and its various forms (the sea, the woods, the night, the winter seasons); the clock as an ever-present reminder of passing time; abstractions or generalities such as Beauty, Death, Pleasure; religious figures such as Christ, Satan and the progeny of Abel and Cain. In some of these cases, no doubt, the poem would have differed hardly at all in its content had it been couched in the third person; but there is, on the other hand, one outstanding instance, that of *Le Cygne*, in which, as we shall see in my next chapter, an initial apostrophe determines the poem's whole structure and even, in part, its syntax.

A particularly striking innovation of structure may be seen in the four 'Death of the Heart' poems: *Causerie*, *Sonnet d'automne*, *Semper eadem*, the second part of *Chant d'automne*. In the first three of these, alternations of standpoint between the two persons involved, are marked by clear dashes; but in a wider sense also, all four poems could be called 'Conversation Pieces'. By this I mean that, in distinction from those many poems in which Baudelaire confines himself solely to speaking his own feelings about the woman he loves, we have here texts which include equally *her* response to him – *her* actual words even, in some cases. This is not to say, of course, that any of these poems are true dialogues; what we hear is still the poet's voice alone, even when he is quoting *her* words or reporting *her* actions or reactions. And yet we do feel as if we were somehow listening in to one half of a telephone conversation: from what we can overhear of the poet's own words, we can infer the response at the other end of the line, we can follow the changes of tone and mood between the two speakers, we can even know what the other's words were as they are repeated back to her by him – even though, all the time, only one voice is audible to us.

This brings me to the question of Baudelaire's undoubted

narrative and dramatic gifts, as shown in so many of these poems. He did of course aspire throughout his life to excel, on a different and larger scale, in full-length novels and plays; but as so often with Baudelaire's literary projects, desire continually outran performance − and besides, Baudelaire's unique talent in his original work lay undoubtedly in the shorter forms: the lyric poem, the prose poem, the novella. (This partly explains his admiration for Edgar Allan Poe, who similarly distinguished himself in the first and third of these genres.) As a prime instance of Baudelaire's talents within the narrower field as well as of his wider if unrealised potential, we may take the first of the two *Femmes damnées* poems − both originally destined, so I believe, to be part of a larger-scale verse novel on Lesbian themes. Already within the purely narrative opening of this poem, each member of the Lesbian pair is superbly and vividly characterised: the strong and dominant Delphine, with her ardent, predatory eyes; the more languid and frail Hippolyte − pallid, numb, sated, uneasy. Beyond this nothing is indicated regarding their identity, and we have no knowledge at all of their origin, their social status, the circumstances of their first meeting, the precise manner in which Hippolyte came to be ensnared within Delphine's toils. And yet everything which is essential to their relationship has been implied in the opening stanzas, or will emerge from the dialogue which follows: Delphine's mature assurance and ruthless, despotic masterfulness, the outraged harangue of her second speech contrasting with the caressing persuasiveness of her first; Hippolyte's sense of an innocence now entirely lost and yet her abiding childlike naivety, her compulsive surrender to Delphine and yet her unbidden stirrings of conscience and her frightened presentiments. Within the whole dialogue, the novelist's gift is preeminently displayed, with each successive speech 'growing' from the one preceding it, or from the relation one to another of the two protagonists within the subtly changing situation in which they are involved. Moreover, not until he judged it prudent to add to this poem, in 1857, five final, condemnatory stanzas, did Baudelaire relinquish the novelist's important commitment to objectivity; until then, he refrained scrupulously from taking sides either against both 'sisters', or for one alone in preference to the other.

The poem *Confession* provides another striking example of these same talents. Within the second and third of its opening stanzas, and with a slow, unhurried accumulation of detail, he contrives to conjure up a whole enchanted nocturnal scene in Paris; then suddenly, unnervingly, the silence of this scene is shattered by the plaintive, strangled cry of distress uttered by the poet's companion – the more startling in that her voice normally rings out so differently: a clear, joyous fanfare in the sparkling, morning air. But now, like some hideous, puny child shunned and imprisoned by its family, and all at once emerging into the outside world, it stumblingly reveals all those deep uncertainties and insecurities that have left their visible imprint behind the lovely woman's radiant exterior. A long pause distances the whole reminiscence; then a final stanza sums up the picture lingering in the mind – with the voice, as one speaks the poem, imposing, in the light of what has preceded, a vibrant emphasis on the single word 'horrible':

> J'ai souvent évoqué cette lune enchantée,
> Ce silence et cette langueur,
> Et cette confidence horrible chuchotée
> Au confessional du cœur.   40

(I have many times cast my mind back to that magically moonlit scene, to the stillness and languor of that moment – and to the terrifying avowal it brought, as the heart whispered its confession.)

Many other examples abound in *Les Fleurs du Mal* of texts in which Baudelaire exhibits evident narrative and dramatic gifts. In his longest and most ambitious poem, *Le Voyage*, a complex framework encompasses both dialogue in the middle sections (between the disabused globe-trotters and the naive would-be travellers) and, at the poem's close, the haunting song of the sirens from beyond the grave, followed by the bracing final apostrophe to Death. *Les Métamorphoses du vampire* prefaces a chilling and desolate scenario with the honeyed, insidious monologue of the vampire-woman; this figure reappears, but now specifically identified with a particular mistress, in the eponymous *Le Vampire*, which is one of a whole number of further poems in vivid dialogue form: *Tout entière*, *La Lune offensée*, *Le Rebelle*, *La Voix* – strictly, a poem of *two* voices, the second only of which, a voice of the Ideal, engages the poet's assenting reply. *Le Vin de l'assassin* ('The Murderer's Wine') is a dramatic monologue – a 'party piece' much requested of Baudelaire the performer of his own poems. I have already referred to the vivid, incidental characterisations offered in *L'Imprévu*, *L'Horloge*, *Don Juan aux enfers*; more extended portraits are presented in *Tristesses de la lune*, *Le Vin des chiffonniers* (the happily drunken ragpicker, re-creating the world in his own image), *Allégorie* (the luxuriantly beautiful woman wholly and professionally dedicated to the cult of Pleasure). Clearly, then, this inveterate self-analyst is also at the same time a 'Man of the Crowd' (the title of a tale by Poe which he translated and echoed in several texts; see *OCP* I, pp. 291–2 and II, pp. 689–90) – the attentive spokesman for many insistent voices from the real or imagined world outside.

Chapter 4

Swan-song: *Le Cygne*

Le Cygne merits detailed analysis as the finest single illustration of Baudelaire's poetic gifts; we may call it his swan-song not only because it has, literally, a swan as its main image and focus, but also because it is the last great poem that Baudelaire completed, in the autumn or early winter of 1859.

The most original feature of the poem, which needs to be recognised from the outset to aid full understanding, lies in its highly innovative structure. In most, perhaps all previously written poems, including those by Baudelaire himself, what is finally presented to the reader is the *rearrangement* in some way (logical or chronological) of the original ideas, the original experience, from which the poem is fashioned; almost by definition there is a gap, more or less wide, between the original sequence of ideas, and the rearranged sequence ultimately laid before the reader. Baudelaire's unusual achievement and innovation in *Le Cygne* is to have *closed* this gap, to have made a poem simply by setting down the thoughts that came freely into his mind at the moment of composition. In so doing, he not only goes some way towards anticipating certain modern techniques ('free association', as pioneered by Freud and his successors; the capturing of a person's 'stream of consciousness', as by Joyce in Molly Bloom's *Ulysses* monologue; the 'automatic writing' of the French Surrealists, in their 'dream poems' of the early 1920s); he also affords us the unique privilege of assisting as it were at the very creation of his poem. This is not to deny, of course, the artistry apparent in his ultimate shaping of this material; however complete may have been his initial surrender

to the flow of his ruminations, in this poetic version he remains continuously and consciously in control, shaping his
text not only to the obvious exigencies of rhyme and metre,
but also (as we shall see) to innumerable other effects of
balance, contrast, harmony, suspense and so on.

'Andromaque, je pense à vous!' In these opening words,
the poet voices his thoughts exactly as they will have occurred
to him, when into his mind there came suddenly the image of
Andromache – in a pose remembered and adapted from a
passage in Virgil's *Aeneid* (III, 294–329); to her, therefore, he
speaks, and to her he will continue, ostensibly, to address all
the ensuing thoughts which in their sequence constitute the
poem. The remembered pose (described in the next four lines)
is of Andromache weeping in exile beside the 'mock Simoïs'
– that mere stream in Epirus to which she had given the
name of the true river sadly recalled from her native Troy; but
these same waters, reflecting her majestic widowhood as she
gazes down on them and as if swelled by her very tears, are
next imagined (line 5) to flow directly into the poet's mind,
there to 'nourish' his already fertile memory – for all the
world like some real river flowing through a rich and green
valley. What here specifically activates (or reactivates) his
memory, as we learn (line 6) at the end of this long opening
sentence, is his awareness of the external scene through which
he is passing: the new, transformed Carrousel square facing
the Louvre, across which (as he has this sudden, as yet unex-
plained thought of Andromache) he finds himself walking,
and which he now infallibly recalls as it once was and as he had
previously known it. But this substitution of the old for the
new, is at first presented in axiomatic, even seemingly sententious terms:

> Le vieux Paris n'est plus (la forme d'une ville
> Change plus vite, hélas! que le cœur d'un mortel) . . .   8

The opening phrase in this couplet is clearly something of a
cliché (like so many phrases that come, unbidden, into one's
mind!); Baudelaire is echoing a familiar and predictable reaction to Haussmann's endless 'renovations' of the 1850s.

But what distinguishes Baudelaire's 'stock response' from that of other contemporary Parisians, is the qualifying parenthesis he goes on to add, under the guise of a paradox which appears simply to be asserting, in the most general terms, that buildings (supposedly so solid and enduring) change in fact more quickly than human hearts (supposedly so fragile and capricious). And yet in its context the aphorism is unmistakably self-regarding: the involuntary 'hélas!' betrays a deep personal commitment to the past, and the plunge into reminiscence in the ensuing stanzas makes fully clear that the unchanging heart referred to is above all Baudelaire's own. In retrospect, moreover, as we shall see, the parenthesis not only qualifies the preceding phrase, it undermines and even contradicts it: the old Paris may have disappeared in reality, but in this particular mortal heart at least, nothing has changed. And so, in his mind's eye ('Je ne vois qu'en esprit', he begins in line 9), as he stands in the new Carrousel and thinks back to the old, the vanished scene slowly re-creates itself, detailed and entire. We see first (lines 9–12) the crowded square, with its chaotic huddle of tumbledown huts and junk-shops, its heaps of unused building materials, its weeds and puddles; then, next (line 13), the menagerie, spreading across a part of the square; next again (lines 14–16), the specific moment fixed for us with some solemnity, with its vague general impression of men going off to work, and of street-cleaners making their 'hurricane' progress through the bright, chilly dawn; finally (line 17), as the poet's thought reaches its point of destination and he is at last able to define clearly what it is that all the time he has had 'at the back of his mind', the single figure of the forlorn swan emerging in all its pitiful and dramatic isolation. There is of course an element of dramatic suspense in the delayed revelation of what exactly it *was* that the poet saw on that far-off morning in Paris: 'Là, je vis . . .' – and then, three lines later, in a place of exceptional emphasis at the beginning of a new stanza, the completed proposition: 'Un cygne . . .', with its ensuing description (lines 17–19) of the swan's plight as it drags its webbed feet and white plumage over the arid pavement. Moreover this 'delaying' device is one that Baudelaire had employed successfully, for specifically dramatic purposes, in several earlier poems: *Une charogne*, *Une martyre*, *Un voyage à Cythère*. And yet, however calculated may be the stylistic effect, the construction equally corresponds, and with singular appropriateness, to the laborious, almost hesitant processes of mental association, on those occasions when we allow our minds to wander, and follow freely yet often gropingly a train of thought leading we know not whither. A similar observation could be made regarding the prosaic, 'modernistic' realism of this whole sequence, on which critics have often commented, and on its audacious, albeit successful contrast with the 'classical' nobility of other sections of the poem. This also, I feel, is too purely literary a reading — for if, as I have suggested, we regard *Le Cygne* as essentially the poetic transcription of a man's thoughts, if we *listen* to it (and no purely silent reading can convey its full resonance) as if to Baudelaire speaking his thoughts aloud to us just as they come into his mind — then we may feel these faithfully descriptive verses to be the obvious and inevitable medium whereby he builds up for us (and, initially, for himself) the accumulating picture that has begun to form in his mind.

With the next line of the poem, in mid-sentence and in a phrase running on from one stanza to the next, a remarkable transformation occurs in the poet's conception and presentation of the swan:

Près d'un ruisseau sans eau la bête ouvrant le bec   20

Baignait nerveusement ses ailes dans la poudre,
Et disait, le cœur plein de son beau lac natal:
«Eau, quand donc pleuvras-tu?, quand tonneras-tu foudre?»

The transformation hinges, it will be seen, on the dual function given to the phrase 'ouvrant le bec'. Initially, this phrase records the swan's gesture of distress, resembling that noted in the next line: the 'bathing' of wings in the dust; it is only when the sentence reaches its climax, in line 22, that this same gesture is retrospectively interpreted by the reader in an-

thropomorphic terms: the swan, it now transpires, has opened
its beak in order to *speak*. It is this anthropomorphic role
given to the swan, which constitutes the transformation
referred to, and thereby marks an entirely new inflection in
the poet's train of thought. The swan is now suddenly
endowed with properly human attributes: a nostalgic longing
for the magnificent lake that was once its home; speech of a
highly rhetorical kind, calling in vain on the thunder and rain
that would bring relief in the urban wastes in which it is
condemned to forage. It is of course very difficult to convey
sympathy with and compassion for the sufferings of animals,
except through anthropomorphic forms of expression – and,
indeed, this tendency is already here displayed, in the
marvellously precise use of the word 'nerveusement'. But
Baudelaire's 'humanisation' of the swan does not spring from
a mere sentimentality; the explanation lies rather in the
ensuing five lines (which conclude the first part of the poem),
and especially in the appositive phrase in the first of these
lines (24): 'mythe étrange et fatal'. From being a mere object
of (deeply felt) compassion, the swan has now, through the
poet's deepening vision, acquired the status of a *myth*; its new
behaviour is entirely appropriate to such a status – for how
else should a mythical swan communicate, save through the
most gravely rhetorical language? And the new role is extended
still further, in the final stanza (lines 25–8) of the first part of
the poem: because the swan's neck strains convulsively *upwards*, towards the sky which by its 'cruel' and 'ironic'
blueness, its settled promise of fair weather, appears to mock
the poor creature's need for rain or water of any kind –
therefore the gesture is seen almost as an act of protest against
an unheeding God.

 The break between parts I and II of the poem, represents
a *pause* in Baudelaire's thoughts: we can imagine him standing
alone in the square, lost in his memories, and then as it were
coming to himself again, gathering his thoughts together as he
once more becomes aware of the present scene. But even in
this renewed awareness, he still remains wholly under the
dominance of the past:

Paris change! mais rien dans ma mélancolie
N'a bougé! palais neufs, échafaudages, blocs,
Vieux faubourgs, tout pour moi devient allégorie,
Et mes chers souvenirs sont plus lourds que des rocs.   32

With this stanza, we are given the full explanation, almost the symmetrical elaboration, of that seeming digression (lines 7–8) which earlier carried us from Andromache to the swan; the cryptic parenthesis which there followed the sententious affirmation: 'Le vieux Paris n'est plus!' (a formula here echoed directly in the words 'Paris change!'), and which lamented the impermanence of buildings when set beside the unchanging constancy of the human heart, now takes on a heightened significance, a more explicitly personal application. The outward forms of Paris may change, but the poet's mood remains obstinately rooted, in its melancholy, to the images of the past he has conjured up for himself; his own heart, indeed, *contradicts* the reality of change, since for him nothing has moved or abated, everything stands unchanged. Or rather, as he goes on to explain, everything, whether old or new, has become for him 'allegorical' – and this is as true of the new palaces in process of construction and of the scaffoldings or blocks of stone still everywhere to be seen, as of the old districts now threatened with destruction if not already destroyed. What Baudelaire means by the phrase 'tout pour moi devient allégorie', can be clearly enough inferred from the poem as a whole: anything and everything that he sees in Paris has the power to call up from the past some related picture in his mind, and such pictures, by their interconnection with others, can serve to crystallise a central emotion or idea, and thereby 'become' an allegory – or a myth (line 24), or an image (line 33), or a symbol ('mon petit symbole', as he was to describe the poem, *CP/* I, p. 623, when sending it in manuscript to Victor Hugo); thus by implication *any* part of Paris he might choose to visit, could stir memories no less profound than those at present aroused by the Place du Carrousel, and could thereby set in motion some further train of 'allegorical' or 'symbolic' associations. As to the adjective 'lourds' ('Et mes chers souvenirs sont plus *lourds* que des rocs'), the next stanza shows this to carry, in retrospect, a

double meaning: not only does it take up again the paradox
of lines 7–8 (mortal hearts are more enduring than cities,
cherished memories 'heavier' than rocks; the immaterial
outlasts, and outweighs, the material); it also hints at all the
dragging sadness that is crystallised, in the line (33) that
follows, in the verb 'opprime': 'Aussi devant ce Louvre une
image m'opprime . . .' This line, as we shall see, is crucial to
the poem's whole development. Already, in the previous stanza, we had begun to see the poet in his role as the solitary
wanderer lost in his urban reverie, for whom the past, sadly,
is more real than the present. Now, additionally, by the syntax and rhythm of this ensuing line, we gain a vivid sense of
approaching climax; suddenly the poet's thoughts have
become clear to him in their underlying and wider meaning,
and with this line begins the long, slow, majestic unfolding of
the idea towards which all his associations and memories have
been obscurely converging. The words 'une image' (line 33),
which at first glance might seem to be referring merely to the
swan which is next evoked, are revealed in retrospect to be of
altogether wider scope: this image that 'oppresses' him as he
stands before the new Louvre, becomes in effect a composite
of *all* those various 'allegorical' or 'symbolic' images –
beginning with Andromache and the swan, but extending far
beyond them – that now begin to crowd into his mind. What
in fact defines this unfolding image is the long sentence that
develops, over the whole of the rest of the poem, from the
phrase (line 34) 'Je pense à . . .' – a phrase that Baudelaire
has already used in the very first line of the poem ('Andromaque, je pense à vous!'), and to which he was significantly
if perhaps unconsciously to revert at the beginning of the letter
to Victor Hugo already mentioned: 'Voici des vers faits pour
vous et en pensant à vous' ('Here are some lines of verse written
for you, while thinking of you') – a phrase that in itself fur-
nishes the whole structure of the last five stanzas, acting as
the hinge on which all else turns, carrying the whole stream
of associations forward, governing almost every subsequent
sentence, whether directly or as an unexpressed antecedent.
Here at last, with his renewed and conjoined descriptions

(lines 34–40) of the swan and Andromache, Baudelaire makes fully explicit to us (and to himself) the link that binds these two figures, and that had remained implicit or purely circumstantial in the first part of the poem. In this second presentation, with its reversed and chronologically more exact order, we note certain significant differences from what has gone before. The two previously separate aspects of the swan are now telescoped into a single impression: the creature is still pathetically 'absurd', with its 'wild gestures', just as in the earlier section in which its physical plight was described with such realistic, almost zoological precision; but also, and in the same breath, it is 'sublime', with its endless and tormenting desire ('rongé d'un désir sans trêve' harks back to 'le cœur plein de son beau lac natal', in line 22) – as befits the humanised 'myth' into which we saw it transformed. A significant interpolation here is the simile which connects the swan with exiles in general – not only (and we must take careful note here of Baudelaire's always deliberate punctuation) because like them it is at once absurd and sublime, but also because, like them, it knows all the torments of longing and nostalgia. In the transition to the next stanza (lines 37–40), continuity of thought and expression are maintained by the run-on effect, which serves also to throw the name 'Andromaque' into high relief, at the beginning of the further tableau which follows. In this, Baudelaire completes the visual impression furnished in the poem's opening stanza, by borrowing one further detail from the *Aeneid* ('Auprès d'un tombeau vide') and adapting another ('en extase courbée'); he also deepens the tragic identity established for Andromache from the outset ('L'immense majesté de vos douleurs de veuve') by recalling the successive stages of her misfortune: widowed by Hector, made captive by Pyrrhus, 'passed on' by him as wife to Helenus (enslavement to a slave, in Virgil's words, *Aeneid* III, 329: 'Me famulo famulamque Heleno transmisit habendam'). But still more striking in its artistry and subtlety, is the way in which, by their pattern, both imagery and sound reproduce or 'echo' the fate of Andromache. I have spoken of the 'high relief' into which her name is thrown by its isolation at the beginning of the stanza: but this is quite literally true, in that through each successive image we are made to follow, as if with our own eyes, that sad *downward* movement: once great herself (as the initial emphasis twice given to her name implies), she *falls* from the arms of her great consort into subjection under Pyrrhus (whose pride humbles hers), and must now *bow down*, in a transport or 'ecstasy' of grief, beside the simulacrum of Hector's tomb; from being great Hector's widow, she has now sadly *declined* to being the wife of the base-born Helenus. So, too, when speaking this stanza, the voice must follow a similar cadence: pitched high on the opening word 'Andromaque', it must then pursue its continuous downward curve until it reaches the final and *contemptuous* enunciation of the three syllables of 'Hélénus'.

I mentioned earlier, as a particularly significant interpolation, the phrase 'comme les exilés' (line 35), which by analogy connects the swan with exiles in general; and this is tacitly confirmed, in the transition to the next stanza (lines 37–40), by the immediate linkage of the swan with Andromache, evoked in her place of exile in Epirus. But it is only when, in the last three stanzas of the poem, we discover these two figures to be the first in a whole long gallery of victims, that we understand exile, in its widest sense, to be the essential theme of the whole poem, the motive principle determining Baudelaire's whole chain of associations:

> Je pense à la négresse, amaigrie et phtisique,
> Piétinant dans la boue, et cherchant, l'œil hagard,
> Les cocotiers absents de la superbe Afrique
> Derrière la muraille immense du brouillard;   44
>
> A quiconque a perdu ce qui ne se retrouve
> Jamais, jamais! à ceux qui s'abreuvent de pleurs
> Et tètent la Douleur comme une bonne louve!
> Aux maigres orphelins séchant comme des fleurs!   48
>
> Ainsi dans la forêt où mon esprit s'exile
> Un vieux Souvenir sonne à plein souffle du cor!
> Je pense aux matelots oubliés dans une île,
> Aux captifs, aux vaincus! . . . à bien d'autres encor!   52

Like Andromache, whom she here follows, the negress (lines
41–4) is a literary recollection – but one deriving from a
youthful poem of Baudelaire's own, recently revised by him
under the new title *A une Malabaraise*. Even more felicitously
than in those earlier versions, Baudelaire now contrives to
amalgamate past and present, reality and desire, within a
single haunting image: the palm-trees of Africa may in reality
be 'absent', but to us as readers no less than to Baudelaire in
his mind's eye, or to the imagined girl in her desperate longing, they are made vividly *present*; the majestic alexandrine of
line 43 replaces them before our eyes, and we feel almost that
they are *there* within her reach, if only she could somehow
break through the imprisoning wall of fog. In her demeanour
and gestures, as she tramples her way through the city mud;
in her physical wretchedness, emaciated, consumptive; in her
awkward subjection to the rigours of an alien climate – in all
these, the negress reminds us of the swan; what links both to
Andromache, additionally, is not merely a common plight
(exile from a cherished land), but also the vain yet pathetic
gesture whereby each in turn seeks to assuage a hopeless longing. Thus Andromache, weeping tears for Hector into the
'false' stream she has renamed in honour of Troy, mimics by
the very copiousness of those tears the realisation of her
desire, and seems almost to achieve the impossible transformation; the swan, mocked by the arid pavement, lost in its
'dream' of deep, native waters, strains its neck in supplication
towards a sky that could bring (but ironically withholds) the
desired refreshment and release; the negress, finally, pursues
with her haggard gaze what her heart tells her *must* lie behind
the vast curtain of fog – as if, into that outward scene, she
could somehow project those exotic palm-trees she has conjured up, as nostalgic 'ghosts', within her own mind.

At this point (line 45), when it might seem that Baudelaire
had identified and drawn together all the diverse threads of
his poem, its perspectives suddenly broaden: individual figures
are succeeded by groups, and at the same time the relationship between these various figures is greatly simplified; a
whole gallery of exiles imposes itself on the poet's mind,

displacing altogether the Parisian scene from which, in the imaginative and associative sense, they have arisen. But the term 'exile' now itself takes on a wider and more inclusive scope; in a formula of marvellous simplicity and poignancy, Baudelaire defines once and for all the wider theme of the poem, the wider range of his compassion: '[Je pense . . .] A quiconque a perdu ce qui ne se retrouve / Jamais, jamais!', ('My thoughts are of all those who have lost what can never, never be found again!') – a compassion that is still further intensified in the remaining lines (46–8) of this stanza, with their deeply expressive articulation of the sense of primal loss, of unsatisfied and eternally frustrated yearning, already so movingly rendered by the simple repetition of the adverb 'jamais'. Perhaps we may feel to be needlessly contrived the 'classical' simile of line 47 (Suffering, by which alone some are 'suckled' or must nourish themselves, pictured as the beneficent she-wolf of Roman legend); yet in the next line, how profound a truth of child nurture, foreshadowing all the discoveries of Freud, Bowlby and others, is enshrined in the touching image of the orphans 'withering like flowers'!

Exile (in both its literal and extended senses); irrecoverable loss or inconsolable suffering of any kind – to these broadening aspects of his theme Baudelaire, in the first couplet of his final stanza, adds yet another: alienation. In so doing, he in effect inserts *himself* within the series; he too becomes a link within the endless chain forged by his reverie. This continuity of thought is not immediately apparent, it is true: the reference to 'un vieux Souvenir' (recalling the 'chers souvenirs . . . plus lourds que des rocs' of line 32), the consequential 'ainsi' (interrupting – and, it would seem, suspending – the long anaphoric sequence which at line 34 had developed from the phrase 'Je pense à . . .') – these might at first suggest some further, interpolated meditation on the processes of memory and change, such as we have twice before encountered (in lines 7–8 and 29–32). But the rhyme-word ('s'exile') clearly identifies the poet himself with all those other exiles, of one kind or another, that he has already enumerated: Andromache, the swan, the negress, the orphaned, the children of Suffering. 'Un vieux Souvenir' (with its allegorising capital letter) refers back, of course, to the poet's recollection of the swan — while linking it with all the other figures which in a less immediate sense are also memories; we are thus reminded of the composite 'une image' of line 33. As to the winding horn-call which figures the distant memory, this suggests (particularly if set in relation with the cognate metaphor in line 40 of *Les Phares*, evoking the lost hunters hallooing from within the deep woodland) a certain *solidarity* of exile and misfortune — betokening as it must another presence in the forest, and thereby, perhaps, some mitigation of solitude, secured through the multiple reverberations of a single 'vieux Souvenir'. But in what way exactly, we must ask, does the poet regard himself as 'exiled'? The simplest answer might be to relate this to the feelings of disorientation and *dépaysement*, the implied resistance to change, that have been aroused in him by the transformation and rebuilding of Paris: on walking through the new Carrousel, he feels himself to be an exile simply because he can never (except in memory) return to the old square that once stood there. 'Exile' in this strictly topographical sense may well have been what first brought the image of Andromache into his mind; now, however, at this final stage of the poem, the concept has been extended to embrace every kind of deprivation and suffering, and has moreover passed beyond the purely Parisian scene. Indeed, if we link the present couplet with the stanza immediately preceding, we may feel the poet to be himself enlisting within each and all of these variously deprived groups: he too has lost what can never be regained, he too has been nurtured by suffering, he too has been orphaned . . . It is certainly significant, in this connection, that in line 36 of a companion poem, *Les Petites Vieilles* (likewise dedicated to Victor Hugo, and published only a few months earlier than *Le Cygne*), Baudelaire should have described himself, in an image identical with that here applied to the generality of life's victims, as 'celui que l'austère Infortune allaita' ('one whom austere Misfortune once suckled'). Equally, of course, if we pay full regard to the reflexive mode of 's'exile', we may feel Baudelaire to be referring simply to his lifelong sense of solitude and 'apartness', as attested by so many texts. On either interpretation, the 'forest' must represent the personal world inhabited by Baudelaire, rather than any more localised setting such as Paris old or new; the horn-call, in its turn, would seem to have the particular function of affirming the poet's *kinship* with that whole community of exiles he has brought together in his mind.

The final couplet of all (lines 51–2) brings a still further widening of this community. From a particular category (the shipwrecked and forgotten mariners) the resumed anaphoric sequence takes us to one so broad ('Aux captifs, aux vaincus!') that one might at first think it to be simply the collective designation, the ultimate summing-up, of *all* the figures previously evoked. For are not Andromache, the swan, the negress, the poet himself, the orphans, the children of Suffering – are not *all* these in some way either 'captive' or 'vanquished', or both at once? But Baudelaire does not choose, or is not free, to end his poem on this note; he is not content merely to sum up, as might be appropriate in a poem of more logical and conventional structure, but must needs follow his train of thought through to its ultimate conclusion – and in so doing indicate to the reader, by the suspensive and infinitely suggestive phrase: 'à bien d'autres encor!', the wider possibilities still that lie open to the truly compassionate mind. It is this opening-out of perspectives at the poem's close, this suggestion of wider ripples and resonances spreading from one victim of exile to another, that give the poem what is to me, together with its originality of structure, its most important quality of all: that of *universality*. Before arriving, with the poet, at this final stage of our journey, we have travelled far in time and space – from classical times to the present day, from Epirus to Paris (old and new), and thence to all the nameless islands and prisons with their store of anonymous victims. But now, finally, having linked in a single compassion so many different figures of misfortune, Baudelaire generalises this feeling to the point where it embraces *any* person or creature destined or condemned to suffer;

from its beginnings in a purely personal and local past, he now extends his vision timelessly into an eternal future. Viewing the poem from our modern perspective, we thus feel it, indirectly, to be speaking to us of *our* problems: by implication, or additional resonance, it becomes at will a poem about Vietnam, the Lebanon, the 'boat people', Kuwait — about any time or place where there are orphans, exiles, captives, vanquished . . . The last five stanzas form, as we have seen, a single, vast, elegiac cadence — but it is a cadence that never quite finds its resolution, since those final words: 'à bien d'autres encor!', with their suggestion of countless further exiles and victims, still leave us in suspense, continuing the poem as it were in our own minds, compelling our attention to the last, challenging and haunting our imaginations; no other ending is conceivable, and none could more effectively conclude (or leave open) this unique transformation of a man's private thoughts, presented in the very form and sequence in which they occur, into a message valid for all times and for all readers.

Conclusion

The paradoxical after-life of *Les Fleurs du Mal*, of which I spoke briefly in my Preface, in effect commenced on the very morrow of the poet's death at the end of August 1867. Simultaneously with the publication by Michel Lévy, only a year or so later, of the *Œuvres complètes* in four volumes (or seven, if one includes the Poe translations), came a remarkably full *Essai de bibliographie* by Albert de la Fizelière and Georges Decaux, and an excellent and reliable biography by the faithful Asselineau. Thus Baudelaire, in his lifetime so vilified by his contemporaries and so misjudged within a narrow-minded legal system, began almost immediately after his death (as was presciently remarked at the time by the original publisher of *Les Fleurs du Mal*, Poulet-Malassis) to be treated as the un-disputed classic of French literature he would eventually become. The essential guardianship of his reputation, from 1887 to the present day, we owe to the Crépet family − first of all, to the pioneering textual and biographical scholarship of Eugène Crépet, who had been associated with Baudelaire from 1859 to 1862 as the editor of an anthology to which the poet had substantially contributed; then, in the first half of the present century, to the massive and meticulous expansion of that work by his son Jacques. Towards the end of his life, in the early 1950s, Jacques Crépet took as his collaborator Claude Pichois − who having become in his turn the undisputed and authoritative master of Baudelairian studies, has been joined recently, as co-author of the long-awaited, definitive biography of the poet, by Eugène Crépet's grandson, Jean Ziegler, thus happily bringing the wheel full circle.

Despite the generally dismissive view of Baudelaire's poetry during his lifetime, he had already begun, after 1857, to exert a decisive influence on a few of his contemporaries – most notably on two of his three great successors in the field: on the Mallarmé of some ten poems of 1861–6; on the Verlaine of the *Poèmes saturniens* of 1866, which owes its very title to Baudelaire's *Epigraphe pour un livre condamné*, as well as of subsequent collections. (For prose eulogies of Baudelaire by these two writers, see Chronology, 1865.) In the poetry of Rimbaud, on the other hand (the third member of the trio), few traces of *Les Fleurs du Mal* are to be found, save in *Le Bateau ivre*; indeed, while hailing its author as a true 'seer', a true explorer of the unknown (in the dazzling discourse on the 'new literature' with which he favoured Paul Demeny on 15 May 1871, as part of the famous 'Lettre du voyant'), Rimbaud goes on to disparage Baudelaire for having failed to match these new themes with the new *forms* they equally demanded. (In point of fact, very soon after this, Rimbaud did in his *Illuminations* find new forms in Baudelaire – but in the Baudelaire of the prose poems and *Les Paradis artificiels*, rather than of *Les Fleurs du Mal*.)

The 1880s and 1890s are the period of Baudelaire's greatest influence in France and French-speaking countries – as may be seen from a number of verse-collections by Symbolist or near-Symbolist poets: Jean Moréas's *Les Syrtes* and *Les Cantilènes*, of 1884–5 and 1886; Gustave Kahn's *Les Palais nomades* and Stuart Merrill's *Les Gammes*, both of 1887; Albert Samain's *Au Jardin de l'Infante*, of 1893; in Belgium, Emile Verhaeren's *Les Soirs* and *Les Débâcles*, of 1887 and 1888. The Symbolist movement itself was launched in the 'manifesto' published by Jean Moréas on 18 September 1886, which took as its basis an interpretation of the first quatrain of *Correspondances*, with its vision of Nature as a 'forêt de symboles' potentially intelligible to Man. What in practice, however, French poets of this period borrow most extensively from Baudelaire, are the portrayal of despairing or nihilistic states of mind – *ennui*, spleen and the like, with many sequences beginning 'Mon cœur est . . .' or 'Mon âme

est . . .', and completed by images taken from sinister or
macabre aspects of external reality; in amorous contexts, the
striking of attitudes in which the woman is seen to threaten
as often or even in proportion as she pleases; the cult of an
aesthetic ideal which by definition remains unattainable; imagery often richly synaesthetic, often tending towards the
crepuscular, the autumnal, the liturgical, the exotic, but at
other times (notably in Verhaeren) harshly descriptive of
great urban concentrations.

In the twentieth century in France, Baudelaire as a poet has
had only one follower of significance: Jean-Pierre Jouve,
who in *Les Noces*, 1931, and *Sueur de sang*, 1933,
recognisably echoes certain themes from *Les Fleurs du Mal*:
evil in woman and as a force in urban society; inner conflict
between spiritual and Satanic impulses. It is a different story,
however, when we come to the critical appreciation of
Baudelaire's poetry. In 1881 and 1883, Paul Bourget had
identified him admiringly as the exemplar of Decadence in
literature – a movement most strongly represented in France
by Huysmans' novel *A Rebours* (1884), with its Baudelairian
hero Des Esseintes. In our own century, creative writers of the
stature of Rémy de Gourmont, Apollinaire, Proust, Gide,
Claudel, Valéry, together with many other critics of any and
every persuasion, united to salute the revered Master; the
literary public, especially after the entry of *Les Fleurs du Mal*
in 1917 into the public domain, in its turn followed more
cautiously but obediently; after the Second World War, the
book penetrated, finally, into academic syllabuses throughout
the world. The annulment in 1949 of the 'condemnation' of
1857 (see Preface) thus came as a sort of official endorsement
of Baudelaire's posthumous rehabilitation, a recognition that
he had at last gained full public approval and even respect-
ability – to the extent indeed of becoming during the 1960s,
for the respondants to a questionnaire in a Paris newspaper,
the supreme French poet of all time. The great commem-
orative exhibitions devoted to his work at the Bibliothèque
Nationale in 1957 and at the Petit-Palais in 1968–9, drew
enormous crowds of visitors, including (in the present writer's

observation) sizeable cohorts of earnest schoolgirls – which would have greatly amused the misogynistic poet who began one of his projected prefaces to the *Fleurs du Mal* of 1861 (*OCP* I, p. 181) with the warning that it was certainly not for his 'wives, daughters or sisters' that his book had been written, any more than for those of his neighbour. But perhaps the supreme encomium came in the 1970s, with the inclusion of the first quatrain of *Correspondances* among the handful of selected specimens of our planetary culture deemed most fitting to be launched into space in a 'time capsule' . . .

In other countries, and especially in England, Baudelaire's growing prestige has been similarly hailed. Perhaps his first foreign disciple was the young Swinburne, who in September 1862 devoted to the second edition of *Les Fleurs du Mal* a highly perceptive review in *The Spectator*, and then in the Spring of 1867 dashed off, in response to a premature report of Baudelaire's death, an impassioned dirge (published the following year) under the title *Ave atque vale*: 'Thou sawest, in thine old singing season, brother, / Secrets and sorrows unbeheld of us . . .' But the *Poems and Ballads*, published in the previous year, concentrate disastrously on those same 'sorrows', *Les Fleurs du Mal* here serving mainly to fuel Swinburne's tediously masochistic fantasies and obsessions, as certain titles within the collection already indicate: *Dolores* (*Notre-Dame des Sept Douleurs*); *Satia te sanguine*; *A Lamentation*; *A Ballad of Burdens*. In the last decades of the century, in England as in France, Baudelaire was much revered and echoed, if no more fruitfully than in the case of Swinburne, by poets of a 'decadent', *fin-de-siècle* tendency: George Moore (*Flowers of Passion*, 1878; *Pagan Poems*, 1881); Oscar Wilde (*Poems*, 1881); Arthur Symons (*Days and Nights*, 1889; *Silhouettes*, 1892; *London Nights*, 1895). One difference between the two countries, however, was that in England the influence continued to be exerted, and more profitably, on poets of succeeding generations – on Imagists such as John Gould Fletcher (*The Dominant City*, 1911–12; *Visions of the Evening*, 1913, with its opening poem dedicated *To the Immortal Memory of Charles Baudelaire*),

F. S. Flint (*Otherworld Cadences*, 1920), Richard Aldington (*Images*, 1919); above all, on the English-speaking poet who is unquestionably Baudelaire's most distinguished twentieth-century follower, T. S. Eliot.

Eliot first registered the impact of *Les Fleurs du Mal* in 1907 or 1908; we can see the indirect but palpable reflection of this influence in the anti-aesthetic urban imagery of *Prufrock* (1919), with its celebrated opening of *The Love Song of J. Alfred Prufrock* — which one may well regard as a modernisation of certain lines in Baudelaire's *Crépuscule du matin* (see pp. 73–4, above):

> Let us go then, you and I,
> When the evening is spread out against the sky
> Like a patient etherised upon a table . . .

Around 1919, Eliot took up Baudelaire for a second time, and by his own testimony 'did not put him down' until 1930; during those years he wrote three authoritative essays on the French poet and referred to him in several other prose texts — rejecting (as Middleton Murry was equally to do, in parallel critical writings) the legend, born in 'the violet-coloured fog of the nineties', of the decadent mid-century aesthete, in favour of a Baudelaire who was a stern moralist and classicist, and what is more (in Eliot's interpretation) a Christian 'born out of his time'. (Two English poets of the previous century, Swinburne and Tennyson, had already been quick to discern the 'moralist' in Baudelaire; see Patricia Clements, *Baudelaire and the English Tradition*, pp. 32 and 64). Above all, in the original manuscript of *The Waste Land* and more sparingly in its final version (with its two 'Notes' directing the reader specifically to *Les Sept Vieillards* and *Au Lecteur*), as well as in several other poems of the period, Eliot develops what Patricia Clements (p. 342) has called his 'wholly personal appropriation of Baudelaire'. Almost two decades later, the appropriation has become so complete as to be almost invisible — as in this passage in *East Coker* which reveals itself on close inspection (Patricia Clements, p. 386) to be an inspired rewriting of the opening stanza of *Le Voyage*:

Home is where one starts from. As we grow older
The world becomes stranger, the pattern more
   complicated . . .
There is a time for the evening under starlight,
A time for the evening under lamplight
(The evening with the photograph album).

Given the favourable reception and eventually more fruitful influence of *Les Fleurs du Mal* in Anglo-Saxon countries, one might well have expected effective support to be forthcoming from competent poet–translators acting as intermediaries. But sadly this has not been the case: there seems indeed to be something about the language and rhythms of Baudelaire's poetry which resists transposition into English verse − so that the reader unversed in French and confronted with versions so entirely bereft of the stylistic qualities of the original, may be excused if he or she is led to question what all the fuss is about, and to wonder whether Baudelaire is anything more than a daring if somewhat *passé* innovator in his subject-matter alone. To gauge the generally low standard of English verse translations of *Les Fleurs du Mal*, one may best turn to the excellent anthology published in 1955 by Marthiel and Jackson Mathews. Showing admirable thoroughness, taste and discrimination in their choice of texts, these two editors have gathered together the best versions they could find of each individual poem in *Les Fleurs du Mal*; it is not their fault if so few of these versions measure up to the minimum standards one is entitled to expect: a rendering of the essential meaning and imagery of the original, couched in idiomatic English; the avoidance of all padding designed to meet self-imposed exigencies of rhyme and metre; above all, the creation of a text which has *independent* value in its own right and its own language. That so few of even the best English versions of Baudelaire's poems (to say nothing of the others) meet these minimum criteria, may be readily verified by reference to the Mathews anthology; I myself would prefer, more positively, to identify the few really good English verse translations which, in this anthology as elsewhere, demonstrate that even the intractable Baudelaire *can* be successfully rendered by poets writing in another language.

By far the greatest number of the texts chosen by Marthiel and Jackson Mathews (some 43 out of 161), are by the South-African-born Roy Campbell; this is not surprising, since he is certainly the most distinguished poet to have attempted, in 1952, a translation into English verse of the complete *Fleurs du Mal*. Yet in this role Roy Campbell has proved boisterously erratic as well as heroic: there is no single unflawed version in his whole volume, let alone among those figuring in the Mathews compilation. Of these, to take two examples, 'Her Hair' (*La Chevelure*) well captures in its opening lines the French poet's fervent rapture: 'O fleece that down her nape rolls, plume on plume! / O curls! O scent of nonchalance and ease!' So, too, the second stanza of 'The Splendid Ship' (*Le Beau Navire*) goes with a fine swing fully appropriate to its theme:

> When you go sweeping your wide skirts, to me
> You seem a splendid ship that out to sea
>   Spreads its full sails, and with them
> Goes rolling in a soft, slow, lazy rhythm.

Yet in both these poems the level, from then on, rapidly deteriorates into artifice and archness. For a complete *Fleurs du Mal* in English, Richard Howard's much more recent version (1982; unrhymed, but in a rhythm which maintains approximate regularity) is greatly to be preferred — even though, here too, the standard varies disturbingly. One complete and sensational success must, however, be recorded; this is 'The Murderer's Wine' (*Le Vin de l'assassin*), from which I reproduce two rumbustious stanzas (the third and fourth) which Baudelaire himself would surely have relished:

> Thirsty — I'm thirsty all the time!
>   A drink is what I need,
> wine enough to fill her grave . . .
>   which means a lot of wine.

> You see, I threw her down a well
>   and afterwards pushed in
> the flagstones piled around the edge —
>   that ought to keep her still.

Returning to the Mathews anthology, this equally brings,

of course, a few (but how few!) versions which are wholly accomplished from beginning to end. By far the most con-
sistently skilful of these translators is F. P. Sturm; of the 19
of his *Poems of Charles Baudelaire* (1906) singled out by the
Mathews, 5 seem to me entirely successful: 'The Remorse of
the Dead' (*Remords posthume*); 'All in One' (*Tout entière*);
'The Sadness of the Moon' (*Tristesses de la lune*); 'A Landscape' (*Paysage*); 'An Allegory' (*Allégorie*). It is significant
that in each of these cases, as also in Karl Shapiro's 'Giantess'
(*La Géante*), Kenneth O. Hanson's 'Spleen' (the first of
Baudelaire's four pieces sharing this title), and Barbara
Gibbs's 'Meditation' (*Recueillement*), the poems translated
are of neater, more studied, more chiselled construction; particular praise, therefore, seems merited by Alan Conder, for
his sensitive and mellifluous version ('Exotic Perfume') of the
more rhapsodic *Parfum exotique*.

I have left until the last, in appraising the Mathews' selection, the one undoubted masterpiece that the translation of
Les Fleurs du Mal into English verse has yielded; what is most
astonishing about this feat is that the poem in question is one
of the longest that Baudelaire ever wrote. The translator here
is Aldous Huxley, and the main title he gives to his version
of the first of the two *Femmes damnées* (*Delphine et Hippolyte*) is simply 'Lesbians'. To give some idea of its quality,
sustained over some 104 lines and almost matching the har-
monious flow yet vivid drama of the original, I must content
myself with quoting the first, third and fourth of its six introductory stanzas:

> The lamps had languisht and their light was pale;
> On cushions deep Hippolyta reclined.
> Those potent kisses that had torn the veil
> From her young candour filled her dreaming mind.

> . . .

> Tears and the muffled light of weary eyes,
> The stupor and the dull voluptuous trance,
> Limp arms, like weapons dropped by one who flies –
> All served her fragile beauty to enhance.

Calm at her feet and joyful, Delphine lay
And gazed at her with ardent eyes and bright,
Like some strong beast that, having mauled its prey,
Draws back to mark the imprint of its bite.

But perhaps, after all, Baudelaire's truest legacy to subsequent creative artists should be sought in another artistic
medium than literature: in music – appropriately enough, in
the case of this poet who especially fostered in certain of his
texts (in prose as well as in verse) the notion of sensory inter-
relationship and of the correspondence one with another of
the various arts. Already in his own lifetime Baudelaire's
verses had attracted the attention of several composers –
among them his (mainly literary) friend aforementioned,
Villiers de L'Isle Adam, whose setting of *La Mort des amants*
excited the admiration of at least one contemporary, Emile
Blémont. But the most justly famous of all songs to words of
Baudelaire's is Duparc's miraculous *L'Invitation au voyage*
– marred only by the composer's strange decision to omit
altogether from musical treatment the second of its three
stanzas. Almost as beautiful are Duparc's other Baudelaire
setting, *La Vie antérieure*, and Debussy's version of *Le Jet
d'eau*; this latter is the third of a set entitled *Cinq poèmes de
Charles Baudelaire* – all five of these poems being among
Baudelaire's very finest (the others are *Le Balcon*, *Harmonie
du soir*, *Recueillement* and *La Mort des amants*): a testimony
to Debussy's unerring taste. But he was then still a young
composer; the other four songs of this set are not quite up to
the standard of *Le Jet d'eau*, lacking its inspired simplicity
and haunting cadences, and certainly do not approach the
uniform excellence of his later and more numerous Verlaine
settings. Another supreme master of the *mélodie* who set both
of these poets was Gabriel Fauré – but his choice of
Baudelaire texts is noticeably less discerning than Debussy's,
and with him, too, subsequent Verlaine groups are markedly
superior. Among the many further French composers of the
nineteenth and twentieth centuries who have set poems of
Baudelaire's, I must mention one recent figure, Léo Ferré,
who hails interestingly from a quite different musical sphere,

that of the *chanson*, and who in his numerous songs from *Les Fleurs du Mal* has shown exceptional sensitivity, intelligence and understanding of prosody. Two particularly successful settings of his are those of *Les Métamorphoses du vampire* (declaimed, in a sinister *parlando*, against a lightly atmospheric background) and of *Harmonie du soir* (an insidious *valse musette*, in appropriately strophic form, with a continually whirling accompaniment in which, as the genre dictates, a piano-accordion predominates). Almost as numerous are the non-French composers who have been attracted to Baudelaire's poems: the Russian Gretchaninov, for instance, in the opening years of the century, selected a whole group; Alban Berg's intricate concert aria, *Der Wein*, linked three poems from the 'Vin' section (*L'Ame du vin*, *Le Vin des amants*, *Le Vin du Solitaire* – 'The Solitary's Wine'), in German translations by Stefan George from his *Blumen des Bösen* of 1901; among the most interesting and inventive settings in our own country are those by Jonathan Harvey, with his cycle for voice and piano to which he has given the collective title *Correspondances*, and which was preceded, several years earlier, by a remarkable melodrama, *L'Horloge*, in which the speaking voice is accompanied by insect-like scurryings on the violoncello. Nor is the musical inspiration derived from *Les Fleurs du Mal* confined to vocal compositions: Debussy's piano Prelude, *Les sons et les parfums tournent dans l'air du soir*, borrows its title from the third line of *Harmonie du soir*; the final movement of Berg's *Lyric Suite*, as we now know, is closely related to the sonnet *De profundis clamavi*; an impressive Violoncello Concerto by Henri Dutilleux takes as its title a half-line from *La Chevelure*: 'Tout un monde lointain . . .', and in the score prefaces each linked movement with quotations from other Baudelaire poems which contributed to the genesis of the piece.

To return to literature, and to conclude: it will be seen that the towering prestige of *Les Fleurs du Mal* is imperfectly measured by its degree of influence upon subsequent poets; but perhaps in the long run this is a boon, since to be poorly

influential is one guarantee among others of secure unique-
ness! This is not to suggest that Baudelaire, any more than
other artists before or since, was independent of the times he
lived in or of his avowed or secret admirations. He was, of
course, above all a child of Romanticism, and in his early art
criticism (the *Salon de 1846* especially) hailed vigorously the
advent of the new era as well as the specific works of Romantic painters. In his poetry he might never, without the example
of such predecessors as Lamartine, Hugo, Sainte-Beuve and
Musset, have taken himself as the prime subject of his poems,
nor the generic Poet as the mythical hero of certain others;
without the stimulus of such lesser Romantics as Petrus Borel
and Philothée O'Neddy he might never have been drawn to
the themes of 'spleen', horror, sadism and the macabre, nor
to dramatise the challenges of particular outcasts (religious or
sexual) hovering on the margins of society. But his self-
analysis, in the detailed and searching intensity of its in-
trospection, goes far deeper than that of any of his precur-
sors; in his exploration of heterodox doctrines and behaviour,
he combines to an unusual degree an obsessive commitment
and sense of identification, with a saving capacity for ironic
detachment and judgment (or self-judgment). Other aspects
of his poetry go back to earlier centuries: his love poetry in
particular revives Renaissance traditions – of tribute,
physical and moral; of less intimate, admirative gallantry; of
reproach, to the unresponsive mistress, from the professional
standpoint of the immortalising poet. But within this
favoured amorous sphere Baudelaire brings also strong personal variations: a fixation with the past rather than with the
present; an ambivalence which mingles (or confuses) hatred
with love; a searing analysis of the destructiveness of passion,
motivating a retreat into safer realms of unassertive
tenderness; a new frankness (rivalling that previously enjoyed
only by painters) in the depiction of erotic seductiveness in
woman and of physical contact between the sexes.

   In many other respects Baudelaire may be seen to modify
or transform what he inherits. In general, in his metrical practice, he shows an abiding concern for established convention

– reaffirmed in an article of 1851 (*OCP* II, p. 39), in which he by implication classes himself among those 'rascals', derided by Ancelle-like notaries, who owe debts and believe that a poet's job is to convey lyrical emotion through rhythms laid down by tradition. But we have seen that his relative conformity in this connection perceptibly relaxed towards the end of his career, when he allowed himself certain audacities in respect of enjambment, of sonnet structure, of stanzaic continuity (the overrunning of one stanza to another in longer poems). However derived and however developed, the sound he brought into French poetry was entirely personal and new, combining the rhapsodic and expansive with the eloquent and dramatic, the bitter and sardonic with the poignant and sensuous. His fondness for certain traditional stylistic procedures: for general and abstract epithets, for allegorical structures and personifications, is similarly individualised; the epithets, by their placing, acquire an uncanny suggestiveness; the allegorical structures take on, as Baudelaire's style develops, a new indirectness and complexity of presentation; the personifications are mysteriously but harmoniously accommodated within contemporary settings. Previous French Romantic poets may have forestalled him in the association of states of mind with corresponding landscapes, real or imagined; but none had developed so extensively as he this art of 'subjective metaphor' – nor again, in another domain only summarily explored before him, of synaesthetic imagery linking impressions from different senses. We have seen that to the theme of Paris Baudelaire gives a new dignity and status, becoming in this respect a 'poet of modern life' to match the 'painter of modern life' he perceived Constantin Guys to be (*OCP* II, pp. 683–724). In the medium of the *transposition d'art*, Gautier especially may have been an influential forerunner; Baudelaire's own essays in the genre, however, confer a new importance on the poet's personal and moral interpretation of the model, extending beyond mere description and aesthetic commentary. Speaking again of Gautier, we may well feel Baudelaire to have admired from the outset that writer's cult of pure form ('l'Art pour l'Art'), as proclaimed in the preface to *Mademoiselle de Maupin* of 1836;

but his own concern for technical finish and virtuosity was practical rather than theoretical, and in any case his conversion, around 1852, to the 'aestheticist' doctrines of both Poe and Gautier, postdates by a good seven years the first composition of most of his poems.

Other features of *Les Fleurs du Mal* seem more purely personal still, in that they lack obvious historical precedents. To the retrospective organisation and presentation of his poems, Baudelaire (ignoring for good reason the conventional chronological arrangement – see p. 6, above) brought a new rigour, a new attention to detail – not only in his pondered choice of main headings and of interior groupings within these, but also in his careful regard for transitions from one individual text to another. An inveterate moralist to the end, he none the less learned to modify his earlier didactic leanings by blending his 'message', in later poems, into a narrative and dramatic framework. With *Le Cygne*, he memorably foreshadows in poetry twentieth-century techniques for transcribing associative thought, and above all attains a universality of utterance rare in any poetry. In his wide choice of subject-matter, finally, he anticipates Realist claims that the artist has complete freedom to write or paint whatever and however he pleases; this freedom applies in detail as well as in general – to individual images, for instance, which may on the one hand be brutally anti-aesthetic, on the other be used to transform the ugly into the beautiful, evil into flowers.

Many of these distinctive qualities of *Les Fleurs du Mal* owe their appeal to us today to the continuing sense of 'modernity' they convey. Certain anticipations by Baudelaire of current preoccupations and vogues may, it is true, seem purely superficial or accidental: the coloured mistress, the Lesbian sequence, the hints here and there (fully amplified, of course, in *Les Paradis artificiels*) of dependence upon drugs. More profound (to pick out some of the most obviously 'modern' of the features noted above) is our appreciation of this poet's lucid and disabused self-awareness; of his understanding of the potential destructiveness of love and of the creative frustrations of the artist; of his eye for the teeming pathos and mystery of city life; of his demonstration that for the poet of sufficient genius, any theme, any technical device, may be fruitful and acceptable. But it is misleading to speak too generally of what is after all a collection of *individual* lyric poems; thus viewed, *Les Fleurs du Mal* is perhaps no more than the unifying framework whereby such texts as *Le Cygne* − in itself a landmark in world literature, valid, as I have argued, for all times, places and readers − may be kept constantly in the public eye (and ear). Like the artists of another individual poem of his, *Les Phares*, who as solitary 'beacons' blaze their defiant message across the wastes of time, Baudelaire the poet is above all the creator of inspired and self-sufficient units, brought together by him to form the composite landmark of *Les Fleurs du Mal*.

Guide to further reading

In the case of items cited more than once hereunder, full details are given at the first mention only. Place of publication, unless otherwise stated or implicit in the publisher's name: books in English, London; books in French, Paris.

Texts

The sole fully reliable texts of *Les Fleurs du Mal* and of other writings by Baudelaire, are those furnished by Claude Pichois in the editions mentioned in my Preface: *Œuvres complètes*; *Correspondance* (*OCP*, *CPl*; two volumes each, both editions published by Gallimard in the 'Bibliothèque de la Pléiade', 1975–6 and 1973, and subsequent revised reprints). The best paperback edition is also by Claude Pichois, in the same publisher's 'Poésie' series.

Verse translations (see pp. 100–3, above): Baudelaire, *The Flowers of Evil*, selected and edited by Marthiel and Jackson Mathews, Norfolk, Conn., New Directions, 1955 (reprint: New York, 1989); Roy Campbell, *Poems of Baudelaire. A Translation of 'Les Fleurs du Mal'*, Harvill Press, 1952; Baudelaire, *Les Fleurs du Mal*, translation by Richard Howard, Brighton, Harvester Press, 1982.

Biography

The definitive biography is by Claude Pichois and Jean Ziegler, *Baudelaire*, Julliard, 1987; an English translation by Graham Robb, somewhat abridged, was published by Hamish Hamilton in 1989. See also the brilliant if controversial *Baudelaire* by Jean-Paul Sartre, Gallimard, 1946; and François Porché's *Baudelaire. Histoire d'une âme*, Flammarion, 1944, which brings many shrewd insights.

Political, social and literary background

D. W. Brogan, *The French Nation. From Napoleon to Pétain, 1814–1940*, Cassell History, 1989; Roger Magraw, *France 1815–1914: The Bourgeois Century*, Fontana History of Modern France, 1983; Charles Morazé, *Les Bourgeois conquérants, XIXe siècle*, Colin, 1957; F. W. J. Hemmings, *Culture and Society in France 1848–1898*, Batsford, 1971; Paul Bénichou, *Le Sacre de l'écrivain, 1750–1830*, Corti, 1973.

Composition

For a detailed account, see Part One, 'The Composition of *Les Fleurs du Mal*', of my *Baudelaire, Collected Essays, 1953–1988*, ed. Eva Jacobs, Cambridge University Press, 1990; for the question of 'l'architecture des *Fleurs du Mal*', see especially essay no. 6, 'Poet – or "architect"?', which gives full bibliographical references. For an account of the trial of August 1857, together with a transcript of its proceedings and of the 'articles justificatifs' by friends of Baudelaire, see *OCP* I, pp. 1176–224; for a full discussion of the background to the trial and of the issues involved, see Jean Pommier, *Autour de l'édition originale des 'Fleurs du Mal'*, Geneva, Slatkine Reprints, 1968.

The French lyrical tradition

By far the fullest and most perceptive survey of the subject is Alan M. Boase's *The Poetry of France. An Anthology with Introduction and Notes*, Methuen. Original edition, subtitled *From André Chénier to Pierre Emmanuel*, 1952; extended edition, in four volumes (I, *1400–1600*; II, *1600–1800*; III, *1800–1900*; IV, *1900–1965*), 1964–73. See also: René Lalou,

Les Etapes de la poésie française, Presses Universitaires de France, 'Que sais-je?' series, 1947; Margaret Gilman, *The Idea of Poetry in France, from Houdar de la Motte to Baudelaire*, Cambridge, Mass., Harvard University Press, 1958; Ferdinand Brunetière, *L'Evolution de la poésie lyrique en France au dix-neuvième siècle*, Hachette, seventh edition, two vols., 1922.

Themes

For general surveys, in their full historical context, of certain themes chosen by Baudelaire, see: Guy Sagnes, *L'Ennui dans la littérature française de Flaubert à Laforgue (1848–1884)*, Colin, 1969; Reinhard Kuhn, *The Demon of Noontide. Ennui in Western Literature*, Princeton University Press, 1976; Paul Bénichou, *Le Sacre de l'écrivain*, 1973; Maurice Z. Schroder, *Icarus. The Image of the Artist in French Romanticism*, Cambridge, Mass., Harvard University Press, 1961; Max Milner, *Le Diable dans la littérature française, de Cazotte à Baudelaire, 1772–1861*, Corti, 1960, two vols.; Pierre Citron, *La Poésie de Paris dans la littérature française de Rousseau à Baudelaire*, Editions de Minuit, 1961, two vols.; David Scott, *Pictorialist Poetics. Poetry and the Visual Arts in Nineteenth-Century France*, Cambridge University Press, 1988.

Critical Studies of Baudelaire's poetry

Jean Prévost, *Baudelaire. Essai sur la création et l'inspiration poétiques*, Mercure de France, 1953; P. Mansell Jones, *Baudelaire*, Cambridge, Bowes and Bowes, 'Studies in Modern European Literature and Thought', 1952; Lloyd J. Austin, *L'Univers poétique de Baudelaire. Symbolisme et Symbolique*, Mercure de France, 1956; Alison Fairlie, *Baudelaire: 'Les Fleurs du Mal'*, Arnold, 'Studies in French Literature', 1960 (and revised reprints); F. W. Leakey, *Baudelaire and Nature*, Manchester University Press, 1969, and *Baudelaire. Collected Essays*, Cambridge University Press, 1990; Richard

D. Burton, *The Context of Baudelaire's 'Le Cygne'*, University of Durham, 'Durham Modern Languages Series', 1980. Most of these books include commentaries on individual poems; see also the notes to the editions of *Les Fleurs du Mal* by Jacques Crépet and Georges Blin (Corti, 1942; augmented reprint, 1950), by Jean Pommier and Claude Pichois (subtitled: *avec certaines images qui ont pu inspirer le poëte*, Club des Libraires de France, 1959), and by Antoine Adam ('Classiques Garnier', 1961 and revised reprints).

Sound and sense

For more comprehensive introductions to the basic principles of French versification, see: Peter Broome and Graham Chesters, *The Appreciation of Modern French Poetry (1850–1950)*, Cambridge University Press, 1976; Ian Higgins, Introduction to his *Anthology of Second World War French Poetry*, Methuen's Twentieth-Century Texts, 1982; F. W. Leakey, *Sound and Sense in French Poetry*, Royal Holloway and Bedford New College (University of London), 1975; Pierre Guiraud, *La Versification*, Presses Universitaires de France, 'Que sais-je?' series, 1970. For two wider and rather differently conceived approaches to the question, see: Clive Scott, *French Verse-art*, Cambridge University Press, 1980; Roy Lewis, *On Reading French Verse. A Study of Poetic Form*, Oxford, Clarendon Press, 1982. For the sonnet in particular, see David H. T. Scott, *Sonnet Theory and Practice in Nineteenth-Century France: Sonnets on the Sonnet*, University of Hull Publications, 1977. For a reading on audio-cassette of 33 selected poems by Baudelaire, according to the principles set out on pp. 52–4, above, see (or rather, hear) *Les Fleurs du Mal*, introduced and spoken by F. W. Leakey, Sussex Video, 1989, FG1A. For detailed studies of Baudelaire's versification, see: Albert Cassagne, *Versification et métrique de Charles Baudelaire*, Hachette, 1906, and Geneva/Paris, Slatkine reprints, 1972; Halvar Olovsson, *Etude sur les rimes de trois poètes romantiques* (Musset, Gautier, Baudelaire), Lund, Bloms, 1924; Jean Prévost, *Baudelaire*, 1953 (chaps.

XXX–XXXII); Graham Chesters, *Baudelaire and the Poetics of Craft*, Cambridge University Press, 1988. For its musical aspects, set in their whole nineteenth-century context, see David Hillery, *Music and Poetry in France from Baudelaire to Mallarmé*, University of Durham Publications (Berne, Peter Lang), 1980.

For Baudelaire's imagery, see Lloyd J. Austin, *L'Univers poétique de Baudelaire*, 1956 (Part Two, 'Symbolisme'). For this and other aspects of his poetic style, see also Henri Peyre, 'L'Art baudelairien', in his *Connaissance de Baudelaire*, Corti, 1951; M. A. Ruff, 'Sorcellerie évocatoire', in his *Baudelaire: l'homme et l'œuvre*, Hatier-Boivin, 1955 (and revised reprints); Alison Fairlie, 'The Art of Suggestion', in her *Baudelaire, Les Fleurs du Mal*', 1960.

After-life

Henri Peyre, 'La Fortune et l'influence de Baudelaire', in his *Connaissance de Baudelaire*, 1951, 'Remarques sur le peu d'influence de Baudelaire', *Revue d'histoire littéraire de la France*, 67, 1967, pp. 424–36, and 'Baudelaire and English Poets', in *Du Romantisme au surnaturalisme. Hommage à Claude Pichois*, Neuchâtel, A la Baconnière, 1985, pp. 167–88; Patricia Clements, *Baudelaire and the English Tradition*, Princeton University Press, 1985; Enid Starkie, *From Gautier to Eliot. The Influence of France on English Literature, 1851–1939*, Hutchinson, 1960; Barbara Meister, *Nineteenth-Century French Song. Fauré, Chausson, Duparc, and Debussy*, Bloomington, Indiana University Press, 1980.

Index of poems by Baudelaire

English versions of titles are given at the first page-reference, except in cases where the meaning is self-evident or is implicit in my subsequent comments.